BOAS & PYTHONS BREEDING AND CARE

by
Erik D. Stoops
&
Annette T. Wright

The beautiful Garden Tree Boa, *Corallus enydris*, a South American native that responds well to captivity. Photo by R. D. Bartlett.

Facing Page:
The Angolan Python, *Python anchietae*, is rarely seen in private collections. It inhabits dry scrublands and rocky expanses in Angola and southwestern Africa. Photo by Roberta Kayne.

1996 Edition

9 8 7 6 5 4 3 2 1   95 789

Distributed in the UNITED STATES to the Pet Trade by T.F.H. Publications, Inc., One T.F.H. Plaza, Neptune City, NJ 07753; distributed in the UNITED STATES to the Bookstore and Library Trade by National Book Network, Inc. 4720 Boston Way, Lanham MD 20706; in CANADA to the Pet Trade by H & L Pet Supplies Inc., 27 Kingston Crescent, Kitchener, Ontario N2B 2T6; Rolf C. Hagen Inc., 3225 Sartelon St. Laurent-Montreal Quebec H4R 1E8; in CANADA to the Book Trade by Vanwell Publishing Ltd., 1 Northrup Crescent, St. Catharines, Ontario L2M 6P5 ; in ENGLAND by T.F.H. Publications, PO Box 15, Waterlooville PO7 6BQ; in AUSTRALIA AND THE SOUTH PACIFIC by T.F.H. (Australia), Pty. Ltd., Box 149, Brookvale 2100 N.S.W., Australia; in NEW ZEALAND by Brooklands Aquarium Ltd. 5 McGiven Drive, New Plymouth, RD1 New Zealand; in Japan by T.F.H. Publications, Japan—Jiro Tsuda, 10-12-3 Ohjidai, Sakura, Chiba 285, Japan; in SOUTH AFRICA by Lopis (Pty) Ltd., P.O. Box 39127, Booysens, 2016, Johannesburg, South Africa. Published by T.F.H. Publications, Inc.
MANUFACTURED IN THE UNITED STATES OF AMERICA
BY T.F.H. PUBLICATIONS, INC.

BOAS & PYTHONS
BREEDING AND CARE

by
Erik D. Stoops
&
Annette T. Wright

Dedication

Through conservation and breeding projects, the boas and pythons of the world may have a new chance to preserve and contribute to the ecosystems to which they belong. Captive breeding and further study of boas and pythons may well be the only way to save them from eventual extinction. Several species are already on their way toward being eradicated.

This manual is dedicated to the individuals and groups who are advocates of the preservation of boas, pythons, and other reptiles of the world.

Contents

Introduction

The Desert Rosy Boa, *Lichanura trivirgata gracia*, has become enormously popular in the herp hobby over the last decade. Photo by R. D. Bartlett.

In recent years there has been a growing trend toward maintaining reptiles in captivity. Boas and pythons are a favorite of collectors since most adapt well to the captive environment. Much research still remains to be done, however, to determine if captive breeding and raising can help to preserve some of the more endangered species. Captive breeding may someday play a big role in determining whether or not entire species even remain in existence.

For example, much destruction of natural habitats is taking place in the forests of Madagascar to make room for human settlements, thus endangering the native species to the point where they may vanish

Dumeril's Boa, *Acrantophis dumerili*, is a resident of Madagascar and closely related to the Boa Constrictor , *Boa constrictor*. Photo by Jim Merli.

completely. Other areas where this process is occurring include Jamaica, Puerto Rico, and the Virgin Islands. Repopulation of the natural habitats with captive-born specimens may not be possible. Thus the only way to preserve some of these species may very well be limited strictly to maintaining the species in captivity.

This book is designed to assist intermediate and advanced hobbyists by providing the basic data necessary to maintain and breed boas and pythons in captivity. The information was obtained from specialists in the field and from our own personal experiences. We have occasionally provided examples of incidents that we experienced and feel no embarrassment in

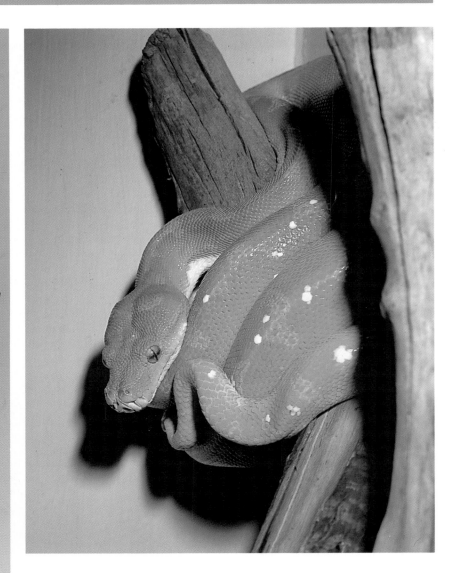

Although primarily an arboreal (tree-dwelling) species, a female Green Tree Python, *Chondropython viridis*, will move to the forest floor in order to lay her eggs. Photo by Roberta Kayne.

admitting our failures as well as successes—this profession is a learning process for everyone, and the sharing of information is vital if we are to participate in the preservation of the boas and pythons of the world.

Using good husbandry techniques is the first step required before any breeding attempts are made. For example, a Green Anaconda, *Eunectes murinus*, must have large accommodations as similar to its natural environment as possible. Some snakes are not as influenced by the environment as others, but any improperly kept snake will be unhealthy and, as a result, will have infertile eggs or stillborn offspring.

Basic Care

VIVARIUMS

Depending on the species, there are several types of vivariums you can provide to assure successful boa and python breeding.

Basic or Exhibition Vivarium: A glass aquarium (or other plastic or glass enclosure) with a substrate of newspaper, pine shavings, or vermiculite works well for many species. Newspaper must be uncolored and allowed to dry in the open air for at least one week to prevent the ink from rubbing off. Wood shavings need to be pine, not cedar, since cedar is toxic to snakes. Vermiculite, a compound made by heating mica, is obtainable through garden nurseries and is the perfect material to use for incubation of eggs and for any snake needing moisture. For example, burrowing snakes such as the Calabar Python, *Calabaria reinhardtii*, prefer a sandy, loose bottom material for reasons of security, and

Many breeders are turning to these modern cages for housing purposes as an option to the more conventional glass aquaria. Photo of an albino Burmese Python, *Python molurus bivittatus*, by W. P. Mara.

With some effort and a little carpentry skill, snake tanks can be made to look as attractive as any other piece of furniture. Photo by Susan C. Miller and Hugh Miller.

vermiculite is exceptional for this need. We prefer to use white cotton terrycloth towels for our substrate, since they can be disinfected with bleach after soiling. Whatever substrate you decide to use, it must be extremely clean and screened to remove insect eggs and larvae. Bedding must be cleaned frequently, particularly the moist spots, since mold and mildew can cause serious skin problems. Other items needed in this type of setup include a sturdy water bowl with about an inch of water, a few pieces of bark or a rock to assist in shedding, a hide box, and, depending on the species, a few branches for climbing.

Desert Vivarium: A few boa and python species require a total desert environment. A glass or wooden enclosure with fine sterile sand as a substrate is best, since these animals need a dry atmosphere. A water bowl may or may not be used; simple spraying is preferred. Potted smooth cacti and various other desert plants can be used

for decoration. (Spiny plants should be avoided.) Examples of snakes that prefer this environment include the Indian Sand Boa, *Eryx johnii*, and the Desert Rosy Boa, *Lichanura trivirgata gracia*.

Woodland Vivarium: Many species of boas and pythons need this type of environment. A glass or wooden enclosure with any of the following substrates works well: green moss, vermiculite, sphagnum or peat moss, or sterile potting soil. The key feature in this type of exhibit is humidity. To retain this humidity, a fine mesh screen or glass top with ventilation holes is needed. Live or artificial plants also help to retain moisture. For arboreal (tree-dwelling) snakes, branches are absolutely essential and can be very attractive. A water bowl and a hide box complete the setup. Examples of arboreal boas and pythons that require this environment include the Emerald Tree Boa, *Corallus caninus*, and Green Tree Python, *Chondropython viridis*. The Blood Python, *Python curtus*, and Amethystine

Making your own tanks can be an interesting and enjoyable experience, but with boas and pythons one must not forget to consider the large space requirements and rigid security measures. Photo by Susan C. Miller and Hugh Miller.

Python, *Python amethystinus*, also prefer woodland vivariums, but care must be taken to prevent the substrate materials from staying damp and molding, since ground-dwellers are more susceptible to skin ailments when the humidity is high.

Expanded Exhibit Vivarium: Large species of boas and pythons such as the Green Anaconda, *Eunectes murinus*, and Reticulated Python, *Python reticulatus*, need large exhibits to accommodate their size. An enclosure made of wood is the most convenient. These vivariums need to be made from smooth-surfaced, untreated woods such as pine. Other types of wood and fabricated wood substitutes can contain many chemicals and can be somewhat dangerous. For example, particle board is toxic due to its glue content. Stains, paints, and varnishes are best avoided, since many produce harmful fumes when dampened or soiled. Many persons experienced in the care of boas and pythons use waterproofing varnishes on wooden cages, but we could find little point in doing this since the risks outweigh the benefits. For an enclosure with a

wooden floor, to prevent moisture from damaging the surface or creating mold, we use plexiglass or plastic sheets over the wooden frame in the construction of the enclosure. Even a plastic tablecloth attached to the floor with double-sided tape or Velcro strips will do. Many people have kept the larger boas and pythons in a room in their home with good results. If this is done, care should be taken to limit roaming to one room and to provide the snake with the consistent ability to obtain heat and water. Depending on the size of the house, even the largest python may need to travel a long distance to find a water receptacle.

Depending on the species, the large, expanded exhibit can be decorated and set up with a desert, woodland, or even a tropical habitat, with large pools for swimming, full-sized trees, and misting systems, and thus create a very attractive system that is similar to the snake's natural environment.

Neonate Vivarium: (for babies and other delicate snakes): By far the most efficient housing method for a neonate (baby) is to use plastic shoebox-sized enclosures

There are many pieces of cage ornamentation available to the boa and python enthusiast, but it is suggested that you acquire those which are easiest to clean. Photo by Susan C. Miller and Hugh Miller.

with beddings similar to what the adults use, but without extra things like plants and rocks. Water bowls should be filled with a maximum half-inch of water to prevent drowning. Some references suggest offering water until the snake drinks, and then removing the bowl, but the question to be raised is: what happens if the snake doesn't drink at your request? Once the neonate is eating and

thriving it can be graduated to a larger enclosure although still smaller in size than what an adult would be housed in. Let them grow into their houses a little bit. The opposite to that is to provide a bigger house before the snake outgrows the old one and can't move at all. For the arboreal (tree-dwelling) snakes, small branches of driftwood can be placed in a shoebox-sized enclosure.

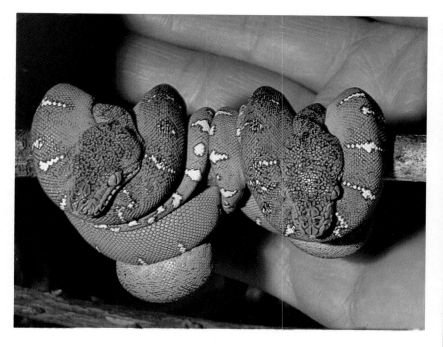

For arboreal species, of which there are many in the family Boidae, branches are an absolute must. Photo of Emerald Tree Boas, *Corallus caninus*, by Roberta Kayne.

They may not be able to hang from it, but they can sit on it and pretend!

FURNITURE

Water bowls, tree branches, plants, and hide boxes are items that need to be placed inside the exhibit. Water bowls ideally should be made of ceramic or heavy plastic material to prevent overturning. The size of the bowl used will depend on the size of the vivarium and the needs of the specific snake. In general, a large ground-dwelling tropical snake such as the Burmese Python, *Python molurus bivittatus*, will need a tub big enough for soaking. For example, a bathtub or plastic children's pool can be used in a room-sized vivarium. Alas, not everyone has an extra room for a bathtub *and* a snake, so a bowl works just as well. Many species are served well with a small bowl for drinking, since not all of them like to take swims. The desert dwellers need to have a dry environment, so the bowl provided should be very small and sturdy. Arboreal boas and pythons spend most of their time in the trees and may not use the bowl for drinking, but will drink off the moistened leaves and sides of the cage. We place a medium-sized water bowl in these snakes's exhibits to help increase the overall humidity rather than to accommodate their drinking and bathing. Tree

There is much time and effort involved in setting up a terrarium as natural as the one shown here, but as you can see, the attractive results are most rewarding. Photo of the Ball Python, *Python regius*, by B. Kahl.

branches for the arboreal boas and pythons should be cleaned driftwood (completely dry without any indication of insects). Artificial plants or live vines have several benefits: Moisture is retained when the leaves are sprayed with water, and they also provide shade and security. Some flowering plants may be toxic to snakes. For example, we were advised by a nursery not to use a Bird of Paradise plant since they are known to be toxic to most animals if ingested, but then why would a snake be eating a plant anyway?

A slightly abrasive rock is useful in any vivarium to assist in the shedding process, although during this process the snake will use the edges of the water bowl or the branches for friction.

SECURITY

All snakes require a place to hide if they feel threatened or stressed. Privacy is essential for successful mating and gestation. The simplest way to provide this is by giving them a hide box. This can be made very simply from a cardboard shoebox or tissue roll, or to be even fancier, from wood, bark, or rock (although be careful of cork, as it is very difficult to clean). Burrowing snakes generally prefer to hide under the substrate on the bottom, and the arboreal snakes like tree branches and leaves the most.

All mating and gestating boas and pythons should be given some kind of box for hiding and nesting. Even if not initially used, it will be available if they need it.

CLIMATE CONTROL

Heat: The average temperature range for most of the boas and pythons is between 80 and 85°F, although some species need very specific temperature ranges. Prior to mating, male boas and pythons usually are cooled to a temperature that is five to 10 degrees less than usual. This is done to increase fertility.

Methods commonly used to provide heat include electrically heated rocks, incandescent light bulbs, electrical heating tapes and cables, under-tank heaters and heating pads, and heat lamps. Whatever method you choose, be very sure to give the snake plenty of room to get completely away from that heat if it wishes.

Heated rocks: These are usually purchased in pet supply stores, and are

Above: Under tank heating pads are becoming more and more popular in the herp hobby. This is a highly reliable source of heating for your boas and pythons. Photo courtesy of Hagen.
Below: Most of the boids are in need of high temperatures if the keeper expects to breed them. Photo of a Boa Constrictor, *Boa constrictor*, by R. D. Bartlett.

The effectiveness of sliding-glass fronts in conjunction with boas and pythons is questionable since they are heavily built animals and could easily smash their way through a thin pane. Artwork by Richard Davis.

more costly than other methods of artificial heating. The advantages lie in their attractiveness, their small size, and their mobility. The disadvantages center mainly around the fact that burns can occur easily since the snakes have to lie directly on the rocks to obtain warmth, and larger snakes can only warm spots of their bodies at one time. Since this is an electrical item placed directly in the terrarium, care must be taken to prevent it from getting wet. Heated rocks should never be used with neonates, since they do not have enough experience to know when to get off them and as a result will become extremely susceptible to burns and dehydration.

Electrical heating tapes and cables: This is a very popular method of artificial heating. It is nothing more than a cable inserted inside a strip of special adhesive tape that becomes warm when plugged into an electrical outlet. It is used on the outside surface of a glass or wooden enclosure or is attached to shelving under the cage. The advantages to using heat tapes or cables are that they can be cut to the appropriate size, thermostats can be easily applied, and they are very efficient in incubators and rack systems designed to

Placing a light bulb on the ceiling of a snake's tank is a perfectly acceptable method of illuminating it. Artwork by Richard Davis.

hold shoebox vivariums for neonates.

Under-tank heaters and heating pads: Obtained in pet stores and hardware stores, these methods are a combination of the previous two. Under-tank heaters are pads placed directly under the bottom panel of a glass aquarium and should not be used in a wooden vivarium. Heating pads can be placed under the cage or inside and covered with the substrate material. The advantage to this method is that a larger area of warmth can be provided. The disadvantage is that if placed in a small exhibit, the area may become too warm, leaving the snake no room for escape.

Incandescent light bulbs (regular type): Light fixtures and 60- to 150-watt light bulbs can be obtained readily in hardware and retail stores. This method of heating is generally inexpensive and efficient for the medium- to large-sized vivarium. The advantage is that the heat is radiant, meaning the general air temperature is affected, thus warming an entire snake rather than just one body part. Also, the lights can be easily mounted inside the vivarium or placed directly on top of a wire mesh screen cover to radiate the heat down into the cage. The disadvantages are that this method not only produces warmth, but also light, which can be disruptive to a boa or python's day/night cycle (photoperiod). Thermal burns can also occur if the snake accidently comes into contact with the bulb, although using a dimmer system with the light fixture will reduce the likelihood of this and assist in controlling the heat output. We once had a Royal Python, *Python regius*, that was so disturbed by the light he struck at it repeatedly and refused to eat although the

method was changed immediately. The lesson we learned was that if a snake objects to a certain item in the enclosure, remove it immediately!

Heat lamps: These should be used only in large, roomy vivariums, and thermostats or dimmer switches should be employed since these produce extreme heat. The bulbs should be reinforced to resist moisture. These should not be used to provide general air warming, like the regular light bulbs, but for spot heating only. This way, plenty of room is provided for relief from the heat.

Humidity: Each species of boa and python has very specific humidity needs,

especially during mating and gestation. Humidity is important for hydration (maintenance of fluids in the body). During mating and gestation, many snakes need to have the rainy season simulated to encourage copulation. The following are some common methods of providing humidity and moisture.

Spraying: Using a plastic spray bottle filled with warm, clean tap water, spray the sides of the enclosure as well as any leaves or branches. Arboreal snakes, such as the Annulated Tree Boa, *Corallus annulata*, will drink this water right from the sprayed surfaces. This method is much preferred

When bringing boas and pythons to shows, swap meets, or even to a friend's house, a simple setup like this plastic sweater box filled with excelsior (thin-stranded wood shavings) will serve the purpose well. Photo by W. P. Mara.

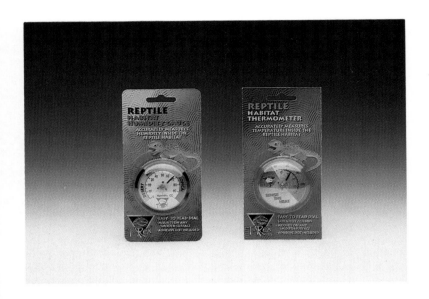

over actually wetting the snake or the substrate. Wet substrates can produce mold, and pouring water on a snake can seriously disturb its metabolism.

Humidifiers: These are electrical devices used to provide room humidity. The advantage in using a humidifier is that a large area can have the moisture level raised, so it is conveniently used in systems with racks of setups. The disadvantage to using a room humidifier is that the moisture can affect the paint on the room's walls, causing mold and bacteria levels to increase. Also, if the humidifier is placed too close to, or actually in, the vivarium, the snake is then exposed to an environment where

bacteria can flourish.

Misting systems: These are commonly used in zoological gardens and are designed for the large vivarium cage. This is a successful means of providing constant moisture and high humidity for tropical arboreal species like the Emerald Tree Boa, *Corallus caninus*, and the various Indo-Australian Water Pythons (*Liasis*). To incorporate a misting system into your vivarium, you can purchase the misting tubing or misting kit at most hardware stores and attach it as directed to a water source. The tubing is attached to the top inside surface. The floor of the exhibit must be raised and a collection system for the excess water placed underneath,

attached to a drain. The floor is best made out of fine wire mesh rather than wood, since wet wood will eventually buckle, warp, or become molded. This can be an extremely attractive showpiece, especially with ultraviolet lighting, plants, branches, etc. The thing to keep in mind is that the misting system is turned on for about 15 minutes at a time, and then the exhibit must have time to dry completely before the next round, approximately three to four days later. Misting usually is done at night to simulate the rainy season, where precipitation occurs right after the normal heat of the day.

Moisture is essential in order to furnish proper breeding conditions. Photo of a neonatal Emerald Tree Boa, *Corallus caninus*, by R. D. Bartlett.

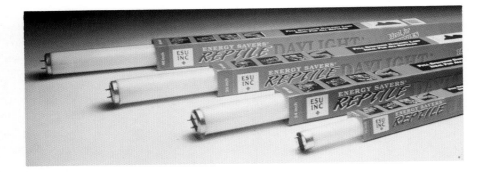

LIGHT

All boas and pythons require ultraviolet light or unfiltered sunlight for proper acquisition of vitamins and minerals in the diet. This aids in shedding and maintaining correct body metabolism as well. Unless you keep your snake in an outside enclosure, you will need to provide an artificial ultraviolet light source. These can be obtained in pet shops. The lights themselves are simple fluorescent tubes but differ through the emission of full-spectrum light including ultraviolet. The light's main benefit is to aid production of vitamin D3 in the skin, which in turn increases calcium and phosphorus absorption into the bones. Vitamin D3 has been studied and is known to play a role in the fertility of sperm, as well as improving metabolism during ovulation and gestation. The light emitted is softer and less likely to disrupt the normal photoperiod cycle of the snake, although it should still be turned off at night.

Photoperiods: This refers to the day vs. night cycle of the boa or python. Nocturnal snakes feed and breed at night; diurnal snakes, during the day. If incandescent light bulbs are used for heating, dimmer switches need to be used to provide dark environments for the nocturnal snakes. Red bulbs are also useful, since they can provide warmth without the bright light. Red bulbs are also very useful with neonates, since most tend to withdraw from bright lights. The hobbyist needs to develop a consistent

Facing Page: Full-spectrum bulbs are important to a snake's well-being and will improve their chances of breeding. Photo of a Boa Constrictor, *Boa constrictor*, by A. v. d. Nieuwenhuezen.

schedule of lighting and darkening the cages. Automatic timers are useful for this.

CLEANING

This is perhaps the most important aspect of proper husbandry. Bacterial diseases can destroy entire collections, and the most common culprit in the spread of disease is the human hand. Your hands should be thoroughly washed between the handling of individual animals since the common bacteria found on the skin of one may be harmful to another. Animals that are unhealthy should be housed in a separate area, as should different species. Substrates should be changed when soiled, and slightly more often if in a high-humidity scenario. The vivarium enclosure and all its accessories should be disinfected when the substrate is changed. We recommend the following: apply one part household bleach in ten parts water, and wait 30 minutes. Then rinse at least three times until no residue remains. We know people who use ammonia, diluted and rinsed in the same fashion, but the long-term results are questionable. Soaps and detergents also should be avoided since they are difficult to rinse out

There are a number of specialized reptile products ranging from vitamins to terrarium cleaners; all have been created to acclimate reptiles to captive surroundings. Photo courtesy of Coralife/ Energy Savers.

completely and residues can be potentially toxic.

Water bowls should be rinsed and filled with clean water every day. Feces (solid waste) should be removed and discarded or an opportunity for bacteria to flourish will exist. This can cause not only health problems, but unpleasant odors as well.

RECORD KEEPING

It is a very good idea for all hobbyists to keep general records about their collections. Some of the topics that should be covered include:

1) Purchase information—when and where the snake was bought.

2) Description of the initial exam—length, weight, general health, and any problems.

3) Records of feedings, sheddings, and any problems associated with these activities.

4) Breeding activities—including when mating occurred, when eggs were laid or live birth took place, and descriptions of the offspring obtained.

5) Illnesses contracted or death. These records can be as basic or as detailed as the keeper wishes. The information is compiled on cards affixed to the vivarium or (if you want to go to the trouble), can be kept completely as computer records. Even

Setting up a regular cleaning schedule and sticking to it is highly advised. Your goal should be to have specimens that look as healthy as this beautiful Ramsay's Python, *Aspidites ramsayi*. Photo by R. D. Bartlett.

When picking up a snake for the first time, or one whose temperament you are unsure of, it is best to grasp the animal behind the head. Photo of Boelen's Python, *Python boeleni*, by K. H. Switak.

Facing Page: If your goal is to calm a snake down, giving it gentle touches can sometimes be helpful. Photo by Isabelle Francais.

the keeper who has just one or two snakes should get into the habit of keeping records in case documentation is needed.

HANDLING

Each individual snake has its own likes and dislikes, as well as its own ideas about what it will or will not put up with when handled. Severe stress can result if a snake is handled excessively or improperly, or if it simply isn't in the mood to be held. Responsible keepers of reptiles will treat a snake with respect and understanding, and in turn will end up with a trusting snake that interacts well with people. Some snakes, like many of the tree boas (*Corallus*), are notorious for being

aggresssive, but even an aggressive snake can be handled if approached and supported correctly.

When you approach a snake, do so slowly, speaking softly and reassuring it, since you never know what sort of mood it's in. We routinely approach our snakes first by speaking to them and touching them softly on the body (having our palm open with the fingers together or our hand fisted in case they do strike in defense). Then, once reassured, we are able to lift them slowly out of the vivarium. If the snake rolls tightly into a ball, tries frantically to get away, or becomes aggressive, continue to reassure it until calm. For boas and pythons in particular, it is

Many people are unaware that some boids have teeth as sharp and potentially painful as any venomous species. Photo an Emerald Tree Boa, *Corallus caninus*, by Robert S. Simmons.

Facing Page: DANGER! Never allow a boa or python to wrap around a child's neck, no matter how "friendly" or "harmless" it may seem. Photo by Isabelle Francais.

best to let them hold on to you since constrictors feel more secure if they have something to wrap around. Support the neck and body, but allow the snake to move somewhat, since any time a snake is held tightly and restrained from moving it becomes defensive and will try frantically to escape.

Snakes typically will move toward the warmest areas at first, then, once warm, will start exploring and moving. Obviously, the favorite place of many snakes is around the keeper's neck or body, since it's very warm in these areas. You should not allow any snake to wrap around your neck,

not only because the larger snakes can cause suffocation, but because even the smaller snakes can cause unconsciousness. This is because stimulation from the snake's coils on the blood vessels of the neck can actually cause cardiac irregularities and decreased oxygen flow to the brain.

There are occasions when a snake must be restrained or controlled, such as during the administration of medications. Care must be taken to hold the snake behind the jaw but not around the neck, and to support the rest of the body as well. Plan to have

two or three people available to help restrain a large snake such as an anaconda *(Eunectes)*. If there is a lack of assistance, try placing the snake in a cloth bag with the head or tail sticking out (depending on which end you are working on) and taping the opening shut. The bag supports the body fairly well, and then all you have to do is control the body part you are involved with. To work on the body of the snake, placing the head in one bag and the tail end in another can work fairly well. The snake is unable to bite, as well as defecate directly on the keeper, which is a common occurrence and one that will win the snake no popularity contests.

For an aggressive snake, the bag method also works well. Encourage the snake into the bag using tongs or a prod. When the snake tries to turn around and escape back out it will pause in its aggression for a short

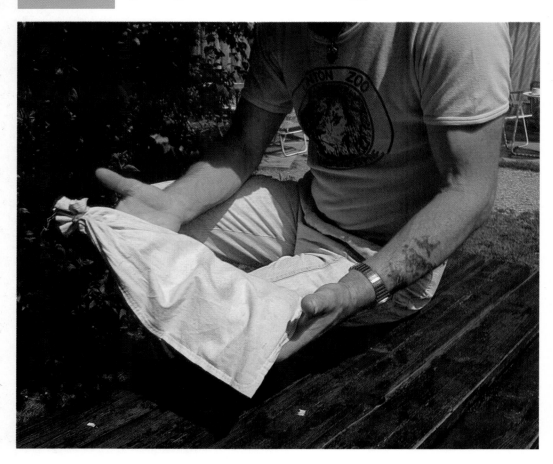

Photo of a young Diamond Python, *Morelia spilotes*, by W. P. Mara.

time. When the head comes out, quickly hold and secure the edges of the bag shut so all that is showing is the snake's head. It will be pretty difficult for the snake to strike, especially if the bag is held in mid-air rather than placed on a table or other surface. You can then proceed to reassure and handle the animal. If the goal in handling is to examine the snake, using a bag made of white or light-colored nylon, or even netting, can be useful.

TRANSPORTING

Transporting of snakes is another form of handling, and one which can result in major stress if not done properly. For shipping via airline or mail services (in the United States and many other countries, it is illegal to send snakes through the federal mail services—though alternative mail services may accept them), the snake should be placed in a cloth bag, then in a styrofoam shipping container and supported with newspaper or cloth to prevent excessive moving/jostling. Shipping is best done at night and should take one day or less since the sooner the snake can be back into its proper environment the less stress will result. We have heard of owners who have shipped snakes without specifying to the shipping

The head is always the first place on which you will want to get a firm grip when handling a boa or python. Many species, this Rough Island Boa, *Canoia aspera*, being a good example, are what some hobbyists refer to as "unpredictable." Photo by Roberta Kayne.

company or airline that the snakes needed to be transported in a timely manner and not left to sit on the concrete outside or in a warehouse for several days. These situations resulted in severely stressed snakes and, in several cases, dead ones.

For short-distance transporting (such as to the vet), you can place the snake in any suitable container, such as a cloth or paper bag, a clean box, or a plastic container (never a plastic bag). Except for cloth bags, you need to provide air holes for ventilation. It is a good idea to spray the snake down before transporting, and if the trip will be long,

bring a water bottle with you so you can spray the snake if it gets too warm or too dry.

A snake or other reptile will tell you clearly when it doesn't wish to be handled, and it is important to pay attention to the signs: tight coiling (Ball Pythons, *P. regius*, are not the only ones that do this), grabbing anything in the vivarium and desperately holding onto it, hissing, frantically attempting to burrow, or striking. If reassurance doesn't calm it, try leaving it alone. Approaching when it's more ready to be handled will give the message that you respect the animal's needs.

Feeding and Nutrition

Photo of the Black-headed Python, *Aspidites melanocephalus*, swallowing a large rat. Rats are a common boid food and can be obtained in most pet stores. Photo by Roberta Kayne.

All boas and pythons kill their prey by constriction. This involves wrapping their bodies around a victim and squeezing until death by suffocation occurs. Photo by A. v. d. Nieuwenhuizen.

Providing good nutrition is a very important consideration when maintaining any snake in captivity. Well before the keeper ever breeds his or her snakes, good nutrition and consistent feeding must be a major consideration. Infertility, unhealthy neonates, and even miscarriages can occur as a result of poor feeding habits early in life. It is in the keeper's best interest to obtain a history of a snake's eating habits, if possible, prior to obtaining the snake. This will determine what kind of nutritional problems they may eventually have to deal with.

Usually a boid will grab a prey item in its jaws and hold it while constriction takes place. Photo by A. v. d. Nieuwenhuizen.

Boas and pythons can easily swallow food items much larger than the size of their mouths. This is done by actually "unlocking" the jaws. Photo by A. v. d. Nieuwenhuizen.

Boas and pythons are constrictors, meaning they kill their prey by suffocation. This activity is often mistaken for crushing or squeezing it to death, which is not totally accurate. By coiling around a food animal, the snake prevents the ribs from moving and constricts the chest cavity so the lungs cannot expand and breathing becomes at first difficult and then impossible. Usually no bones are broken in the prey. Once the prey is dead, the snake will consume it whole. There is no possible way that a snake can chew, tear, or otherwise alter the prey,

Often a boa or python will consume an entire meal in a matter of minutes. Photo by A. v. d. Nieuwenhuizen.

Many keepers prefer to give their snakes frozen-and-thawed mice rather than live mice. Frozen mice are now available in packages at many local pet shops. Photo courtesy of Ocean Nutrition.

Facing Page: Mice, along with rats, are probably the most commonly offered captive snake food. They form a complete diet for boas and pythons and are easy to acquire. Photo by Michael Gilroy.

so the proper-sized food must be offered.

FOOD PREFERENCES

Boas and pythons consume a variety of prey, such as rodents, frogs, lizards, and birds. In captivity, a diet of rodents is preferred by most keepers, keeping in mind that some boas and pythons have particular tastes and preferences. Mice and rats, as well as chicks, treefrogs, and small lizards, can all be purchased. "Pinkies" are newborn rats, mice, or gerbils, "fuzzies" are older rodents that do not yet have the eyes open but are just beginning to get hair, and "weanlings" are baby rodents that have just been weaned.

HOW MUCH HOW OFTEN?

When talking about how much to feed a snake, it is much better to give them several small food items rather than one large piece. Neonates require small items once or twice a week due to their rapid growth and metabolic needs. Juveniles should be fed once every seven to nine days. They are notorious for acting extremely hungry all the time, even if fed heavily. The keeper who overfeeds a juvenile for any reason is risking the health of the snake. For example, we know of situations in which keepers have fed Burmese Pythons so much that in one year the snakes were approximately 10 to 12 feet long, which is of

course absurdly large for a yearling. The snakes were easily induced to mate, but had infertile eggs since full sexual maturity is not reached in most boas and pythons until at least 18 to 20 months of age, regardless of size.

For adult specimens, feeding frequency depends show no adverse effects. Ball Pythons in particular often concern their keepers by refusing to eat for months on end. Food should be offered on a regular basis because eventually the snake becomes hungry again.

The other consideration that the keeper must

An aggressive bird-eater, the Emerald Tree Boa, *Corallus caninus*, has been known to sit atop tall trees and actually "pluck" victims in mid-flight. Photo by Jim Merli.

on the metabolism of the particular species. For instance, heavy-bodied snakes such as Ball Pythons, *Python regius*, need to eat a lot less often than an active snake, such as a D'Albert's Python, *Liasis albertisii*, which has a higher metabolism. Some species can even go several months without eating and decide on is whether to feed live or pre-killed prey. Live prey in a vivarium may be looked upon by the snake as an invader, so the snake may strike and kill it in defense but then not consume it. The keeper must also be aware that a live prey animal, particularly a rodent, may become

One of the few truly aquatic boids, the Green Anaconda, *Eunectes murinus*, has a highly varied diet that includes fish, small turtles, and even small caimans. Photo by Jim Merli.

aggressive toward the snake as a result of fear and cause severe injuries. On the other hand, some snakes may refuse to eat a pre-killed item despite all attempts to make it more appealing.

If the keeper decides to use pre-killed food and the snake has demonstrated a desire for it, then the best way to obtain it is through one of the many frozen, pre-killed food dealers. If this is not possible, the keeper can humanely sacrifice live prey himself by simply freezing it. Many references advocate other methods, such as stunning the prey by hitting it on the head, which works but doesn't seem very kind

(and there is still a potential for injury to the snake if the prey animal becomes alert again), but freezing has always worked best for us.

Most boas and pythons will develop a recognizable eating pattern early in life. However, on occasion a keeper will come across a situation where their snake(s) will simply refuse to eat. There are a variety of reasons why this might happen, and troubleshooting the problem can be very time-consuming.

Boas and pythons may refuse to eat if the temperature and/or humidity is not appropriate, if the vivarium is not clean, if they are preparing to shed, or if they are stressed. Some even have preferences as to which time of day they will accept food, the location in the vivarium where the food is placed, or even the method in which it is provided (such as with tongs vs. the keeper's fingers).

For example, we were contacted by a desperate associate who was unable to get his juvenile Ball Python *Python regius,* to eat. We interviewed him and found that he was feeding his snake by

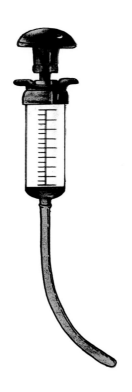

A typical force-feeding syringe. Although usually effective, force-feeding is a stressful procedure for a snake and should only be used as a last resort. Artwork by Scott Boldt.

removing the water receptacle as well as the hide box, and then dangling the pre-killed rodent in front of the snake. We suggested that he leave the water bowl and box in the vivarium, since these are familiar items to the animal, then put in the food item and simply leave everything alone. This worked very well for that particular python, since it was very shy.

Some keepers routinely feed their snakes outside the vivarium to maintain cleanliness, a procedure we do not advocate. For some boas and pythons this is a threatening

procedure since they are away from their familiar surroundings. Some snakes have such a sense of "home" that they will actually move the food into their hide box prior to consuming it.

FORCE-FEEDING

If loss of appetite becomes prolonged and results in malnutrition with loss of weight and development of lethargy, the keeper may need to force-feed the individual to maintain its health. Force-feeding is a delicate process that should be done by an experienced individual. When a snake eats normally it has to unhinge its jaw to accommodate the body of the prey, slowly working the item down the esophagus into the stomach by means of rhythmic contractions of the muscles in the neck and upper body. The food is lubricated with saliva as it is taken into the back of the oral cavity.

In force-feeding, the snake is made to open its mouth by applying slight pressure on the hinges of the jaw. This is usually done by inserting a narrow, flat object, such as a tongue depressor, between the upper and lower jaws. Extreme care must be taken to prevent injury to the jaw and neck, since the snake invariably will resist this procedure.

The food is best administered in liquid or semi-liquid form by use of a syringe, pump, or a tube attached to a syringe. Attempting to place a whole, solid food item in the mouth is much more difficult since snakes are very good at spitting such things out. "Pinkie pumps"

preparations, fluid and electrolyte solutions, and even medications, can easily be administered through a syringe attached to a tube inserted into the back of the oral cavity, or even by syringe only, with the food placed in the mouth. The snake can then "drink" and swallow the preparation with little effort. Once the food is far enough back into the

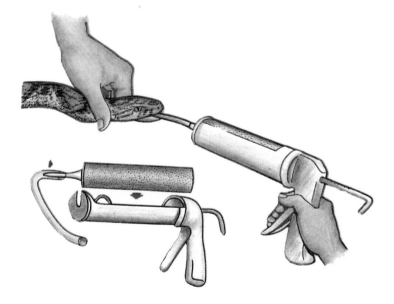

Some hobbyists choose to make their own force-feeding apparatus by using an old caulking gun. This illustration also shows the correct way to grasp a snake's head during the gun's usage. Artwork by John R. Quinn.

(special syringes that chop up, liquefy, and deliver food items into the snake's throat when pressure is applied to the pump) are commercially available. Any food that is even semi-solid must be lubricated with water or a sterile water-based lubricant to assist in passing the food into the stomach. Liquid

throat it proceeds fairly easily into the stomach. This way the snake does not have to expend as much energy unhinging the jaw, and the muscular contractions needed to mobilize the food are lessened.

Our favorite food preparation is made by mixing pureed beef or

Feeding newborns can be a very frustrating affair. The keeper may have to try a number of different items. Photo of neonatal Garden Tree Boas, *Corallus enydris*, by R. Allan Winstel.

chicken, small quantities of bone meal and vitamins, and raw egg with a fluid containing electrolytes. This is very easily administered by syringe and is perfectly acceptable to the snakes to which we have given it.

The keeper needs to keep in mind that the snake is stressed by any method of force-feeding so it should be given small amounts at a time and then allowed plenty of rest. Once it begins to regain its strength, the keeper should attempt to feed it in a normal fashion, allowing it to consume the food voluntarily.

FEEDING THE YOUNG

The initiation of feeding in neonates (babies) is a challenging skill that can be very time-consuming. After the neonate sheds for the first time, a small food item can be offered. The keeper may not have any success getting it to eat for up to a week after the shed, since it is still being nourished by the embryonic yolk absorbed prior to birth. Some neonates are hearty eaters and will accept pre-killed food items, but others are very particular and may want either live food or particular items such as frogs or lizards to start with. Their willingness to

Newborn snakes usually will not eat until after they have had their first shed. Photo of hatching Diamond Python, *Morelia spilotes*, by Paul Freed.

eat also has a lot to do with their environment since young snakes typically are shy and often defensive.

A common practice in feeding a fussy neonate is to rub the food item with the entrails of a more preferred type of prey, such as a chicken or lizard. We commonly do this with all our neonate Green Tree Pythons, *Chondropython viridis*, as well as with the Emerald Tree Boas, *Corallus caninus*, since they repeatedly insist on having their pink mice or rats "scented" at first. For those neonates that insist on live food, the prey should be young itself to decrease the chances of it attacking and injuring the snake in question.

If all attempts to feed a neonate fail, force-feeding may have to be tried. All you have to do is take a close look at how very small and fragile a neonate is to realize how delicate a procedure this will be. Feeding liquid or semi-liquid preparations via small syringe or very fine tube is the only truly safe method. The amount needs to be extremely small and carefully adjusted since ruptures of the gut can result. The risk of injury and death is great due to the stress and

The Burmese Python, *Python molurus*, has a voracious appetite, which is a characteristic one should look for in any pet snake. Photo by Roberta Kayne.

fragility of the subject, so only experienced professionals should attempt this.

Malnutrition also can be a serious problem. This includes the snake that is overfed and obese, as well as one that is not fed enough and thus is emaciated. Existing health problems, such as bacterial infections and parasites, can cause malnutrition, and these conditions must be diagnosed and treated promptly if the snake is expected to breed and produce healthy offspring.

Health Problems

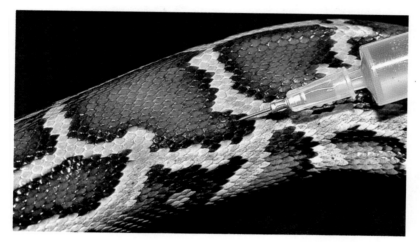

If and when a boa or python needs an injection of some sort, it should be administered by a qualified professional *only*. Photo by Dr. Fredric L. Frye from *Reptile Care*.

Prevention of health problems is an important aspect of good husbandry. Fortunately, most of the common problems are easily dealt with, but it's important to understand the causes in order to prevent them in the future. Taking care of health problems is a learning process that all hobbyists are involved in at one time or another. A veterinarian experienced in the care of reptiles is a good resource when attempting to locate the cause of the problem, as well as in treating the more complicated diseases.

We would like to point out at this time that we have given some examples of our own experiences and remedies in the following sections. We are not veterinarians, and the doses and specific uses of certain compounds were not always determined by a vet. Unless you are willing to essentially put the snake's life in your own hands, it is best to consult a professional before using any chemical compounds.

ISOLATION OF WILD-CAUGHT SPECIMENS

When purchasing a boa or python, captive-born specimens obtained from a reliable source are less likely to have any serious health problems than those taken directly from the wild. If you obtain a wild-caught animal, it

Occasionally a captive snake will indeed die, and when this happens it is best that the keeper preserve the body for future examination. Photo by Dr. Fredric L. Frye from *Reptile Care*.

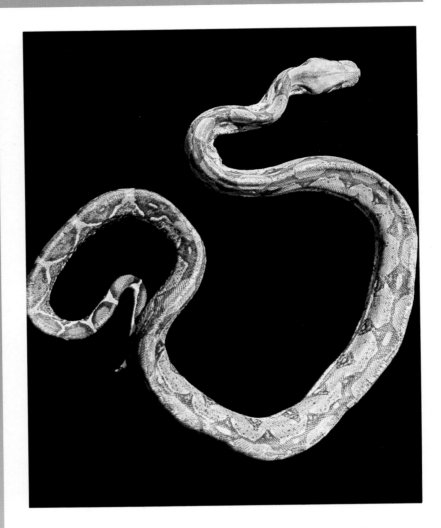

should be isolated in a separate room for about a month for observation before introducing it to other members of the collection.

STRESS

Stress is one of the major killers of reptiles. It is caused by improper husbandry techniques, improper handling, and improper transporting and shipping. It will cause health problems such as greater chances of bacterial diseases, and these in turn will further the stress. This vicious cycle has resulted in many reptiles otherwise known for their captive hardiness suddenly doing very poorly.

A stressed snake will not eat, becomes lethargic, shows poor color, and has vomiting or diarrhea. To treat the animal, a proper environment must be provided. Exact

Burns can cause a snake great pain and may leave permanent scarring in their wake. Photo by Dr. Fredric L. Frye from *Reptile Care*.

temperatures and humidity for that particular species need to be set up in an appropriate cage. These snakes should not be handled and should be given a liberal degree of privacy.

BURNS

Thermal burns are a common occurrence when a reptile comes into contact with a heat source for a long period of time. Burns appear as red or gray swollen or blistered areas. The scales may be totally eliminated in a serious burn, leaving the skin grayish and shiny. Overheating, although not actually a burn, is just as serious. The snake that is overheated will be agitated and constantly try to find shade or water to relieve the pain. A seriously

Severe skin conditions should be treated with the utmost dispatch. The ensuing stress alone is often enough to cause death. Photo by Dr. Fredric L. Frye from *Reptile Care*.

overheated or burned snake will twist its entire body or even lie belly-side up. Long-term overheating, especially with neonates, results in bone deformities. To treat an overheated snake, place it in a lukewarm water bath, *not* a cold one. The water gradually will lower the body temperature and provide fluids and electrolytes to combat the associated dehydration. For burns, the skin must be gently cleansed every day with plain water. Topical ointments (applied on the skin) will coat the burn while healing takes place. During the healing process the temperature should be 75 to 80°F, and all materials should be kept clean and dry to reduce the likelihood of infection.

TRAUMATIC LESIONS (BITES)

The most common lesions are from the bites

Deep cuts and gashes like the one shown here often are the result of fights with cagemates or aggressive prey items. Photo by Dr. Fredric L. Frye from *Reptile Care*.

Since boas and pythons are so large and powerful, they can easily smash through aquarium glass if given good reason. Wounds resulting from such an accident often will have to be sutured. Photo by Dr. Fredric L. Frye from *Reptile Care*.

of prey; especially rodents. When considering feeding, pre-killed food is to be preferred. Firstly, the live prey is an invader to the snake's territory and the snake may become defensive and stressed as a result. Secondly, if the snake hesitates or strikes in defense, the prey, especially a rodent or lizard, may bite back. To prevent this from happening, use pre-killed food or monitor the feeding situation very closely. Be prepared to remove the prey if the snake doesn't appear hungry. Never leave unmonitored live prey in the cage overnight!

Bites can also occur when the keeper feeds more than one snake in the same cage simultaneously. The rapid movements of one snake capturing prey can be misunderstood by the other snake(s), and striking/biting may occur.

There are many products available to improve the health of captive herps. Vitamins are essential in keeping healthy large boids. Photo courtesy of Coralife/Energy Savers.

Facing Page: Note the head scales on this Green Tree Python, *Chondropython viridis*. This is what the scales on your own snake's head should look like. Photo by Jim Merli.

Also, when the keeper allows contact with other domestic animals, like dogs or cats, problems can occur. This is an excellent reason why it's always best to keep a snake in an enclosed vivarium rather than left to roam freely. Bites can be as small as a puncture wound or as large as a tear. Severe bites can be deep enough to expose muscle tissue. A snake that has been bitten will be severely stressed and agitated. The bite usually will bleed freely and is thus easily identified. Cleaning the wound daily with plain water and applying a topical ointment will assist healing.

Vitamins must be added to the diet to promote proper skin and tissue healing although scarring is not preventable. Severe bites should be treated by a veterinarian since many require surgery and/or special dressings.

One unfortunate occurrence that happens every so often is when two or more snakes try to ingest the same prey. Never attempt to pull the snakes apart. Simply submerge them in a water bath and they will separate voluntarily. To prevent this in the first place, feed all snakes separately.

POISONING

There is a long list of substances toxic to snakes, whether by ingestion, breathing fumes, or via skin contact. The general rule is to avoid using a chemical in the vivarium or in the general location of the vivarium

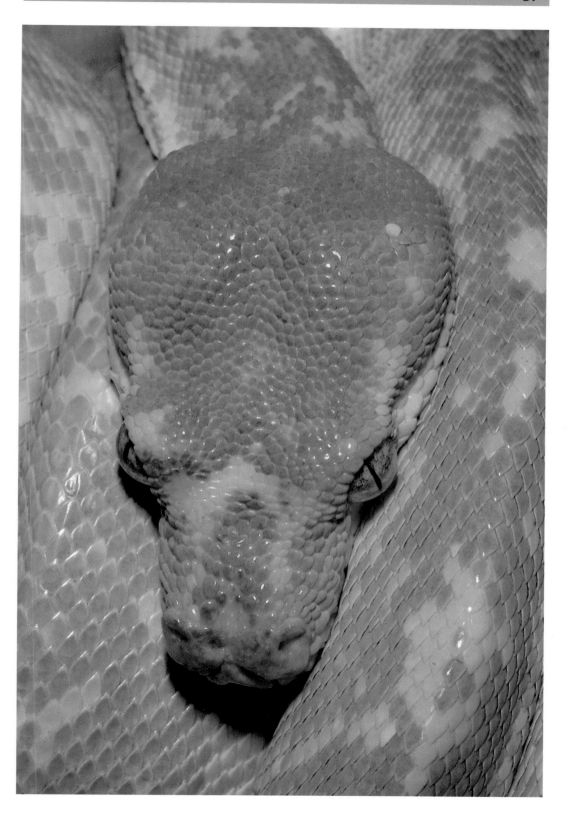

Mites and ticks should be checked for regularly. Photo of the Madagascan Boa, *Acrantophis madagascariensis*, by K. H. Switak.

unless it has been documented safe for reptiles. Some of the more common substances that create problems are powders, ammonia, soaps, pesticides, glue, and particle board.

We would particularly like to mention the use of applies to sticky "glue traps" and fly papers used to control pests. Neonates and small snakes can actually get caught on the sticky material and die.

Some chemical substances, such as bleach, can be used as treatments for certain

"pest strips" (insecticide-impregnated plastic) for medical purposes, which seems quite popular these days. These should never be placed inside the vivarium. The same diseases (through cleansing, etc.), but these should not come into actual contact with the snake. The general rules to consider when using any substance are: to use

One of the most productive places to look for mite and tick infestation is on the head. Photo of Dumeril's Boa, *Acrantophis dumerili*, by Roberta Kayne.

only small amounts on an occasional basis, dilute solutions with water to make them less concentrated, and be sure to rinse the chemical off unless it is a medication that is not meant to be rinsed or diluted (such as antibiotic ointment).

VOMITING AND REGURGITATION

There are several factors that can encourage vomiting. Stress due to excessive handling, improper environmental temperatures, and overfeeding are the main ones. After any kind of transport, snakes should not be fed for at least seven days to allow rest and reorientation. Water should also be provided during this time.

Extreme temperatures may also cause vomiting. After eating, snakes should not be handled for at least 24 hours. Handling them at such a time can not only cause vomiting but may injure the distended intestines. Feeding the snake large amounts of food or large prey animals can cause overdistension and regurgitation. Snakes being treated with antibiotics may regurgitate repeatedly due to elimination of the normal bacteria present in the gut, which does not allow proper digestion. If vomiting occurs, allow the snake to rest several days before trying to feed it again. If using pre-killed food, make sure it is warm to the touch and fresh. Finally, give the animal plenty of privacy and time.

CONSTIPATION

Depending on the activity level and general metabolic (digestive) rate of the snake, defecation (elimination of waste) may commence anywhere from two days to three to four weeks after consumption. Some snakes defecate almost exclusively before shedding and do not show any signs of gastric distress as a result of the delay. Signs of constipation, therefore, are not strictly dependent on timing but on actual signs of distress such as bloating, lethargy, and refusal to eat.

The best treatment for constipation is to bathe the snake in warm water. For severe constipation resulting in ruptures of the abdominal wall, the same treatment is useful, except you should make sure the water is sterile. (Obviously your vet should check such a snake and suggest a more effective treatment.) We've heard of

instances where a constipated snake was given rectal stimulation with a probe coated in glycerin, which resulted in further trauma and injury to the rectum. Check with a qualified professional before taking this procedure any further.

RESPIRATORY PROBLEMS

Respiratory problems occur as a result of

Respiratory illnesses commonly are the result of poor husbandry, particularly from drafts and a lack of appropriate heat. Snakes like this young Rainbow Boa, *Epicrates cenchria cenchria*, need a fairly high temperature in order to thrive. Photo by R. D. Bartlett.

bacterial or viral infections and can be brought on by the trials of stress. Cold stresses due to improper heating techniques, as well as the stress of transport, predispose the snake to respiratory ailments. There are several different organisms that cause infections of the respiratory tract, but the signs and symptoms are universal: coughing and wheezing, nasal discharge, open-mouth breathing with frothing of saliva, refusal to eat, and other signs and symptoms of stress. The snake may lie on its side due to respiratory distress, and swelling around the lung areas may be noticed.

If your snake shows any signs of a respiratory ailment, it is very important to immediately

isolate it to another room. Employ meticulous hand washing between handling since this ailment frequently is contagious.

The treatment for this problem is to first provide a temperature of 85°F and to make sure the environment is dry. Placing a small amount of eucalyptus oil in a container and putting it in the vivarium will relieve some of the obstruction and allow the snake to breathe easier. Extreme privacy is essential, since these snakes are highly affected by added stresses such as noise or handling. Antibiotics such as ampicillin and amoxicillin can be administered,

aquarium with a branch and a small water bowl. The substrate provided was sanitized cotton towels. To provide warmth, we placed a heating pad under the glass bottom and a heat lamp above the vivarium. The temperature was controlled at a constant 85°F. Towels were placed over the top and front both to provide privacy and to help maintain the warm, dry environment within. The snake was given 250 mg of ampicillin in a fluid containing electrolytes, administered orally two times a day. A few drops of eucalyptus oil were placed in a small container and then the container was put in the vivarium. The treatment was continued for seven days, after which time the wheezing and coughing were absent, but we kept the "patient" in the enclosure for an additional seven days for further observation. No further problems ensued so the snake was returned to the rest of the collection, taking food without further difficulty.

Even for snake species that need high levels of humidity, warm, dry air is necessary to decrease bacteria levels for healing to take place. This particular snake

preferably by the mouth, although some references advocate injections.

An example: Our Emerald Tree Boa, *Corallus caninus*, which was imported from South America, was noted wheezing and making oral "popping noises." It was isolated and placed in a regular 10-gallon glass

Make it a habit to regularly check around the nose and mouth for any signs of discharge, etc. These often are the first signs of a respiratory problem. Photo of the Jamaican Boa, *Epicrates subflavus*, by R. D. Bartlett.

voluntarily drank water and, once treated, was placed back in the usual misting/spraying cycle. Some respiratory diseases left untreated can result in, among other things, pneumonia, so it's important to treat them early.

OTHER BACTERIAL CONDITIONS

Salmonella: Although a lot less common than it once was, salmonella is still an occasional problem. Snakes, as well as other reptiles, can carry salmonella organisms and should have a stool culture done by a veterinarian to rule out this disease.

Infectious Stomatitis ("Mouth Rot"): This is the most common of all snake diseases. The bacterium involved invades the soft tissues of the palate and eventually spreads to the bone, destroying teeth, gums, and jaws. Many references suggest that poor husbandry practices such as unclean vivariums and stale water play a big role in how susceptible a snake is to mouth rot. Other causes, such as injuries resulting from striking at hard objects, rubbing the mouth and

This photo amply shows the oral signs of an extensive case of infectious stomatitis, otherwise known as "mouth rot" Photo by William B. Allen, Jr.

Ventral view of a preserved specimen of *Boa constrictor melanogaster*. Photo by J. K. Langhammer.

nose areas against metal cover materials, and general stress, all increase the likelihood that the snake will contract the disease. The signs of mouth rot include the gums and lips becoming swollen and grayish in color, and a perpetual opening of the mouth. If left untreated, the infection spreads rapidly and can advance to such a severe state that the esophagus and intestines will be infected as well. Care must be taken to isolate the animal affected. Measures such as wearing gloves and frequent hand washing must be observed to prevent the spread of the bacteria to others in the collection. The following is an example of treating this ailment when it occurred with one of our Emerald Tree Boas, *Corallus caninus*. Imported and quarantined for a long period of time in questionable conditions, the animal had a severe case of both mouth rot and dehydration, and as a result it became severely stressed. The first thing we did was to provide fluids, electrolytes, and a proper isolated environment. Hydrogen peroxide was

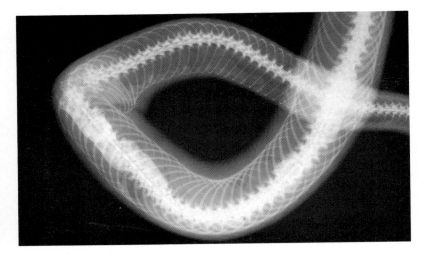

X-ray showing broken bones of a small snake. With quick and immediate medical attention, even a severe fracture like this one can be treated with full expectation of recovery. Photo by Dr. Fredric L. Frye from *Reptile Care*.

Facing Page: Preventive measures are the only form of medicine a keeper should practice regularly. Having specimens as healthy as this Rainbow Boa, *Epicrates cenchria*, should be the main goal. Photo by B. Kahl.

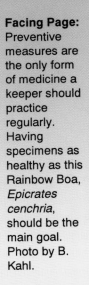

applied by a cotton swab to all surfaces in and around the mouth, which upon close examination appeared to have a large amount of "cheesy" material adhered to it. We of course cleaned this area completely.

Then we noticed a large number of missing teeth, but were not concerned since teeth will grow back once the tissues return to normal. Sulfamethazine solution was applied via syringe to all the surfaces of the inner mouth and gums. This adheres to and kills the bacterial colonies. Next we mixed 125 mg of ampicillin with 500 mg of powdered ascorbic acid in an electrolyte solution and administered it orally to the snake. The entire treatment was given twice a day for seven days, after which time the snake appeared to have recovered completely, but for reasons of assurance we continued to observe it for recurrences of the problem for an additional week.

If the symptoms don't subside in the first week, treatment can be continued for up to 14 days. Avoiding additional stress is very important, so the snake should not be forced to eat until the treatment is complete. If the snake is in such poor condition that it cannot wait to eat, vitamin supplements and pureed meats, such as those found in baby foods, can be fed via syringe at the same time the medications are given. Every three to five days is fine.

Blister Disease: Blisters can occur as a result of too much moisture in the substrate in conjunction with mold or bacterial colonies. Unclean substrates are the medium in which bacteria grow

well. Usually noted on the ventral (belly) scales of the snake, blisters are filled with pus and can become so extensive that the scales and tissues underneath abscess and become necrotic. A snake with blisters will show the usual signs of stress and refuse to eat, as well as have twitching movements and agitation. If not treated, blister disease can spread to the nasal, oral, and anal cavities and can even cause death.

We successfully treated a case of blister disease in a Green Tree Python, *Chondropython viridis*, by the following method: Our gravid female was in a nesting box for a long period of time, on a substrate that included lots of green moss. This produced undesirable amounts of excess moisture and caused blisters to form on the scales along the ventral surface. The first part of the treatment was to remove all the old substrate material and sanitize the vivarium completely. The existing substrate was replaced with sanitized white cotton towels. The general temperature and overall humidity were carefully monitored. Each individual blister was given the following treatment: First, it was gently rubbed with a moist cotton swab along the edges, resulting in rupturing of the blister. The fluid inside each blister escaped and the surface was cleaned with half-strength hydrogen peroxide. This cleansing does not harm the snake and is necessary to assist in the drying process. A solution of one part povidone/iodine solution to four parts sterile water was applied to the affected area and then allowed to dry. This was done once a day for 14 days, during which time the blisters dried and scabbed over. The snake went into an opaque state (prior to shedding), then shed on day 21, having some flaking of the skin along the affected areas. Voluntary feeding occurred, and an additional shed was executed approximately 30 days later. At this time the infected areas were noted to have healed. The eggs produced, however, were infertile. We believe this was due to the stress of the affliction rather than to the treatment provided. If the treatment had not been employed, we would have lost a fine member of our collection, and the loss would have obviously been much greater.

A good place to look for the early warning signs of many diseases is in and around the oral cavity. Photo of a Boa Constrictor, *Boa constrictor*, by Jim Merli.

Occasionally, for no known reason, fluids collect beneath a snake's brille and can result in a disfiguring bubble in the eye. When properly treated by a veterinarian, as shown on this and the facing page, the condition may be cured in just a few days with no permanent harm to the animal. Usually the vet will remove the fluids by way of a very fine syringe. Obviously, a hobbyist should never try such a procedure. Photos by Dr. Fredric L. Frye from *Reptile Care.*

Abscesses: These occur as a result of trauma such as burns, bites, etc., as well as parasites. The lesions from these injuries become infected, harden, and then spread into the muscle tissues and internal organs. The nodule contains hardened debris that must be removed to allow healing. Surgery is only occasionally required, mostly for extremely deep visceral abscesses (extending into internal organs), and should only be done by an experienced veterinarian.

The usual treatment is to make an incision and drain the abscess, then apply hydrogen peroxide solution for thorough cleansing. Applying diluted povidone/iodine solution and then a topical antibiotic ointment will assist in the healing process as well. Like all health problems, stressors

such as handling and excessive light should be eliminated, and the animal should be observed closely for any further problems.

EYE PROBLEMS

In the snake that is generally dehydrated and/or emaciated (very thin), commonly the capsule of the eye collapses inward and appears sunken. A successful method for treating this condition is to hydrate the snake with electrolyte solutions and water administered orally by syringe or by tube feedings. Treating the underlying dehydration for at least seven days usually will result in rejuvenation of the capsule.

NORMAL SHEDDING PATTERNS

A snake is essentially an organism made up of body parts contained in a continuous cylindrical

container. The outside layer of skin sheds, while new skin grows underneath. In effect, the snake grows inside-out just as we do, but in their case it is a much more obvious process. When that outer layer is removed, the process is known as ecdysis, molting, or **shedding.**

Normally, the process involved is as follows: Prior to actual shedding, the

say, this is the time when snakes are most protective of themselves. Being blind and having very delicate skin to protect, they become more defensive and aggressive yet are lethargic. This is the time the snake is most likely to strike at you. This period lasts from seven to ten days, during which time the animal will most likely refuse to feed. Captive-born specimens may eat

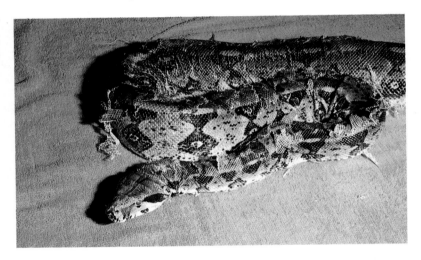

Trouble with shedding is a common problem among snakes, especially those in captivity that are not given a water bowl, rock, and/or branch. All these items assist them during a slough. Photo by Dr. Fredric L. Frye from Reptile Care.

new skin develops under the existing layers. The general color of the old skin will appear duller than usual but still remain supple, not dry. The eyes are covered with a transparent scale, the brille or spectacle, which also becomes cloudy, appearing bluish white in color. This opaque covering limits the snake's vision to the point where it becomes nearly blind. Needless to

during this period, but probably shouldn't do so since stretching of the new, tender skin may disrupt the development process. Feeding a live prey animal during this time is especially dangerous. We have seen several instances in which the snake killed the prey strictly in defense, without eating it. This was of course a waste of food and completely without benefit

to the snake in question. Naturally, the other danger to consider is the fact that since a snake cannot truly see during this time, any rodent that decides to fight back probably will win. The result of that occurrence doesn't really need to be stated here.

During this time, provide privacy and avoid handling. Frequent spraying of warm water onto the sides of the vivarium is needed to increase the general humidity, since the snake may refuse to move even enough to drink. Some snakes may sit for long periods in a water bowl and must be monitored for decreased temperature and problems associated with increased moisture, such as blister disease.

During the actual shedding process, a snake usually breaks the nose and throat skin by rubbing against rocks, branches, or any other item it feels is adequate. It continues to crawl out of the existing skin from the head to tail, turning it inside-out in the process. If all goes well, the old skin will be in one complete piece.

If a boa or python has difficulty with its shed, there is nothing wrong with a keeper helping it along. Larger species can actually be brought into a bathtub filled with warm water and the old skin removed by hand. Photo of *Candoia aspera* by Paul Freed.

A rapidly growing juvenile will tend to go through this process more often than an adult, but there is much variation in all individual snakes as to how often.

SHEDDING PROBLEMS

Problems associated with shedding occur when the skin sheds in patches or strips, or the eye scales or anal plates remain fused to the new skin underneath. The main reasons for improper shedding include dehydration, lack of adequate ultraviolet light, skin lesions associated with trauma or disease, and poor husbandry.

Improper Shedding (Dysecdysis) of the Brille: The brilles are the most crucial part of the shed. The snake does poorly if it is unable to see to locate prey. We have heard of instances where brilles were not removed after six or seven sheds. This of course can lead to a whole variety of problems, slow destruction of the eye being one of the more common ones.

Removing the brilles manually is a very sensitive process, since the tissues are very delicate. After soaking the snake in warm water for eight to twelve hours, use a cotton swab moistened with sterile water and very gently rub along the edges of the brille and socket. If the scale refuses to come off, apply warm, moist compresses over the eyes and try again. If that doesn't work, try rubbing the area with mineral oil

A snake will look its best when shedding is finished and all skin has been removed. Photo of the Timor Python, *Python timorensis*, by R. D. Bartlett.

and again try to remove the scale. If that too fails, a veterinarian should be consulted; he may remove the eye plates with forceps. Keep in mind that the surface of the eye is directly under the plate and can be damaged if an amateur tries to use forceps on his own. Any snake that has several layers of brilles remaining should also visit the veterinarian so the eye can be inspected for damage or infection after the scales are removed.

A heavy branch, like the one this Banana Boa, *Ungaliophis continentalis*, is resting on, should be included in every snake's tank. Snakes depend on rough surfaces like these to begin their sheds. Photo by Roberta Kayne.

Dysecdysis of General Skin Surfaces: The reason for treating this problem and manually assisting the snake to complete the shedding process is because if the skin sheds in patches or strips, bands of dried skin can potentially constrict the blood flow to vital areas. Dead skin also can cause irritation and increased susceptibility to bacterial skin diseases. The main component in treatment is to provide hydration of the skin as well as friction to assist the removal of the patches. Soaking the snake in a water bath of approximately 78 to 80°F for eight to twelve hours will hydrate the skin. Then, place the snake between layers of toweling to provide friction and rub gently, starting at the head and moving toward the tail.

Here is an example of an improvised method we have successfully used on members of our collection; it is particularly useful for venomous snakes and neonates: Place moistened green moss as well as a small amount of sphagnum (peat) moss in a cloth bag and place the snake inside for six to eight hours. The bag itself will provide friction and moisture as well as security. Since air flows freely through the cloth, there is less concern over excessive moisture contributing to skin

lesions. As the snake crawls through the moss, it picks up moisture and has plenty of friction to remove the dried skin. When removed, the snake is completely relieved of the patches. In several instances, the eye and anal scales also were completely removed. We've used this method on neonates, which can drown if placed in a water bath. We've also used it for several adult specimens of the genera *Python* and *Corallus*, with excellent results. This also is a perfect setup for any venomous or easily stressed reptiles, since there is safety for the handler as well as security for the animal.

Providing humidity as well as adequate ultraviolet light on a steady basis will prevent improper shedding in most cases. Lesions such as blisters, burns, bites, etc., even though healed, can still result in improper shedding even after healing, but later sheddings usually will be free from incident, providing the healing is complete. Scarring can sometimes cause improper sheds, and the above treatments may need to be employed. It is very important to provide surfaces that assist the snake in shedding (i.e., abrasive rocks, etc.).

This photo should give you some indication as to just how large a tapeworm can be. Imagine the damage it could do when inside a snake
Photo by Paul Freed

PARASITES

Internal parasites:

Tapeworms and roundworms are fairly common internal parasites that invade the digestive tract. Most boas and pythons are fed a diet of complete animal carcasses, which can easily host developing parasites. Snakes that regularly take live prey are more susceptible to these conditions, but even captive-born animals that are fed pre-killed food can contract worms if the food is diseased.

It is highly recommended that the keeper who obtains a wild-caught snake have a stool sample checked under a microscope (by a veterinarian) to test for the presence of parasites. At least tapeworms and some roundworms should be detectable. The snake should be isolated from the rest of the collection until the testing is complete, since any type of parasite is potentially contagious to the others. Any snake showing the following signs and symptoms should be isolated and a stool sample checked: vomiting, diarrhea, dehydration, bloating, emaciation unusual resting behavior such as lying on the back or side, or signs of extreme stress. When fed, infected snakes will often eat very rapidly, but vomit within the next 24 hours.

Tapeworms are actually made up of dozens of smaller segments that can break off and operate independently. This particular specimen was taken from a Green Anaconda, *Eunectes murinus*. Photo by William B. Allen, Jr.

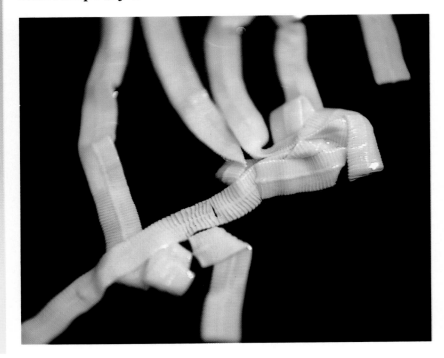

Removing a tick can be a very delicate affair. There are lances that are safer to use than the knife shown here. Photo by William B. Allen, Jr.

The treatment of these parasites has two very important components. Firstly, supporting the overall condition of the snake is important, since infections cause rapid debilitation due to malnutrition and dehydration. Eliminating stress is again a major factor in successful treatment, and the snake needs to be protected from any added stress such as noise, bright lights, handling, etc. To combat dehydration, electrolyte solutions are administered orally.

Secondly, once the parasite has been isolated and identified, anthelminthics and other medicines

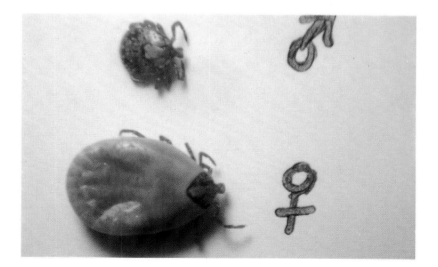

Ticks can come from any number of places and should be removed immediately. Photo by Dr. Fredric L. Frye from *Reptile Care*.

Shown here is a very healthy example of the Rubber Boa, *Charina bottae*. Note the clean scales and rich coloration. Photo by Ken Lucas, Steinhart Aquarium.

Mites can be found in a number of places in one's home, i.e., baseboards, attics, and cluttered cellars, and may leave these spots to crawl onto a captive snake. Photo by Dr. Fredric L. Frye from *Reptile Care.*

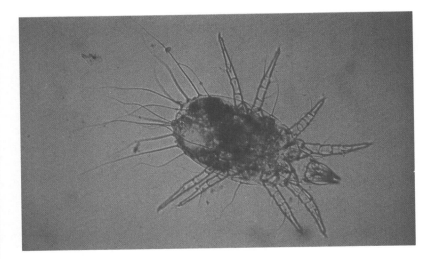

should be obtained from a veterinarian. They will provide dosages based on weight and general condition. You should administer these as directed, giving electrolyte and vitamin replacements at the same time. Some keepers advocate the use of standard worming medications designed for dogs or cats, increasing the dilution of the medications for safety. This is fairly risky, since the medications themselves can cause additional problems and may not be specific enough to destroy the parasite involved.

External Parasites: The most common reptile health problem is the external parasite, i.e., mites and ticks. These are found in most outdoor areas, but also colonize indoors. Baseboards, damp or dusty corners, cluttered areas, wood

Sometimes a colony of mites will not be spotted for quite some time because they can hide and breed in substrates like wood shavings or bark nuggets. Photo by Fredric L. Frye from *Reptile Care.*

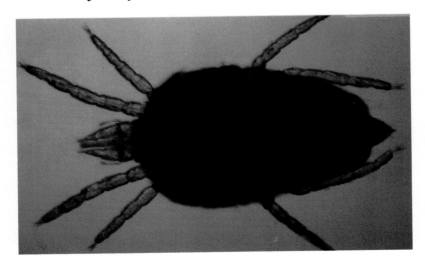

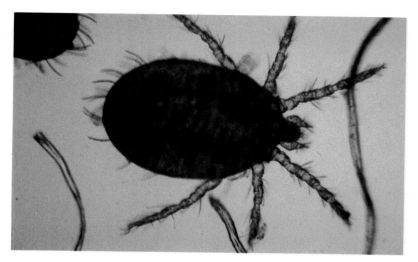

Mites often will hide themselves so deeply on an animal that they will not be noticed until the problem has grown completely out of control and extensive damage has already been done. Photo by Dr. Fredric L. Frye from *Reptile Care*.

cracks or crevices, and any other dark, moist environment can be a home for these creatures. Any material that's brought into the snake's environment, such as rocks, driftwood, substrate materials, plants, as well as any crevices in the vivarium structure itself, may serve this purpose.

Mites and ticks are attracted to snakes because their scales provide them with a place to grow while they feed on the snake's tissues. The most common places to find mites or ticks on a snake are under the large scales on the ventral surface, on the chin, and around the mouth and nostrils. You also may see them residing in the eye sockets, vent, and heat-sensing pits. Mites appear as very small black dots. Ticks are much larger and

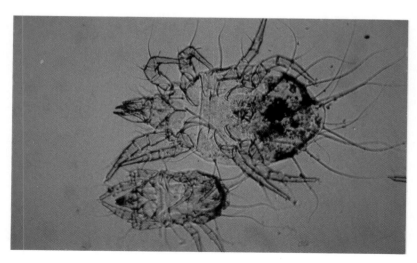

A keeper should inspect all of his or her animals at least once every two weeks for signs of parasitic infestation. Photo by Dr. Fredric L. Frye from *Reptile Care*.

usually red or brown. Mites are nocturnal and can be seen migrating over the snake's body when it's dark. Mites can cause extensive scale damage and scarring, as well as small hemorrhages in the skin tissues.

A snake with mites or ticks will be restless or agitated, may twitch or shiver, and frequently will soak itself in water in an attempt to remove them. If the parasites are located on the head, you will notice the snake rubbing its snout, eyes, or mouth against objects in an attempt to relieve the irritation. In severe infestations, snakes will show definite signs of stress and as a result may refuse to eat.

Mites (and less so ticks) rapidly migrate from one vivarium to another, so successful treatment needs to involve both the whole collection and the general locale. The most common treatment advocated is to place the individual snake in a water bath of 70 to 75°F for 12 hours. The mites usually will drown and fall to the bottom of the container. Afterward the substrate needs to be changed, and all materials inside the vivarium, as well as the cage itself, should be thoroughly sanitized.

The disadvantages of using this method are that the mites may not all drown, since some will migrate to the dorsal (top) surface of the snake when

A keeper should be careful when handling any snake since a mite or tick infestation can just as easily attack a human. Photo of Boelen's Python, *Python boeleni*, by K. H. Switak.

it floats. Also, not all of the eggs are destroyed using this method either. Lastly, soaking the snake for long periods can cause problems with the skin in general.

We have used a successful, though controversial, method for eliminating those mites and ticks that are not treatable by water immersion. We place the snake in a completely dry container or paper bag and dust it with approximately two to three tablespoons of garden carbaryl insecticide. The "patient" remains in this container for 24 hours, after which time we remove it and proceed to rinse off the powder. Extreme care is used to prevent it from drinking during the rinse—hold its head down and support the closed jaw. Thorough cleaning of the vivarium is done during this time. The snake typically sheds seven to ten days after this treatment.

A lesson we learned, however, was that it is equally important to sanitize the floor, walls, and other places (like baseboards) to prevent recurrence. If possible, it is a good idea to treat the entire collection, or at least the snakes in the same general area, at the same time. Otherwise, you may end up chasing the parasites from one cage to

Pine needles might make an attractive substrate, but they also provide a perfect home for mites and ticks. Photo of the Desert Rosy Boa, *Lichanura trivirgata gracia*, by R. D. Bartlett.

When working around the head while applying creams, ointments, or whatever, be sure to avoid unnecessary contact with a snake's eyes. They are among the most sensitive areas on its body. Photo of *Loxocemus bicolor* by Roberta Kayne.

another, accomplishing very little. The dusting method we use kills the eggs, and the fumes released in the container kill the adults before they can escape. However, this dusting technique is probably too toxic for neonates and juveniles, for which we use the bathing method.

To avoid all the hassle involved in treating this condition, prevention is of course the key concept. Using sterile substrates and sanitizing all materials coming into the vivarium is essential. You should routinely quarantine any new snakes obtained, and treat them if necessary. The room housing the collection should be free from clutter, and the floors and walls should be dusted and sanitized frequently. If furred animals are present, they should be dusted with flea and tick powders appropriate for the species.

Many keepers advocate the use of sticky pest strips in the general location of the vivariums. These are strips of sticky material attractive to flies, fleas, and the like. Care must be taken to avoid using them in the vivarium itself, since even the ones without pesticides can be toxic in an enclosed, moist environment.

HEALTH PROBLEMS ASSOCIATED WITH BREEDING

Mating Ritual Injuries: In large communal vivariums where several pairs of boas or pythons are kept together, or in situations where two males are placed together, certain injuries can occur. Some species of boas and pythons will conduct a "mating dance" in which males will combat and the dominant male at the end will breed with any or all of the females he chooses. Injuries that can occur include bites between males, but more serious are tears from the bone "spurs" located on either side of the vent opening. Occasionally, similar injuries will occur between mating pairs if the female is resistant to the male's attempts to mate, so breeding should be monitored closely. Spur injuries are much more prevalent between males, however, and can do serious damage. To control this, proper sexing of the pairs needs to be done, and two males should not reside together once they are sexually mature (since fights can occur even without a female in attendance). In the communal situation, monitoring of all breeding activities must be done so that the keeper can separate the antagonists before actual injury occurs.

For example, several pairs of Cook's Tree Boas, *Corallus enydris cooki*, were kept together in a large communal vivarium and allowed to breed as if in their natural environment. The following occurred: Two males moved to the bottom and began twisting around each other in an attitude similar to mating, but advanced quickly to a combat situation. The sharp bone spurs caused lacerations when the ventral surfaces rubbed against each other, and biting and hissing occured as well. The females remained on the upper branches, but became agitated. One male dominated the other by actually pushing his opponent's body into the substrate and holding him down for a short period of time. Then the dominant male released him and climbed back onto the branches, mating with the females. Due to the extremely rapid progression of the combat, as well as the degree of agitation from all the snakes, we were unable to separate the antagonists until the combat was completed. Both males were inspected for other injuries, and the lacerations and bites were

Pregnant snakes are, as one might expect, highly susceptible to health problems, and thus should only be handled when absolutely necessary. Photo of a gravid Desert Rosy Boa, *Lichanura trivirgata gracia*, by K. H. Switak.

treated appropriately. The males were separated permanently after this incident. We have even heard of an instance where the lacerations were so severe the snake in question required 40 stitches.

Egg Impaction: During the egg-laying process a snake often becomes stressed and/or fatigued, especially if the eggs are larger than usual or are turned abnormally in the oviduct. This fatigue will diminish the strength of the contractions, and the eggs will remain inside the body. An impacted egg can cause serious complications, such as spoiling of the egg and bacterial infection of the oviduct, if not removed immediately. A snake with impacted egg(s) will be of normal girth (size) above and below the impaction, and extremely distended just above the vent area where the impaction is located.

Manual assistance must be given. There are two ways to do this: 1) massaging the impaction and gently working the egg(s) toward the vent, which is the most common method of treatment), or, 2) coating the vent opening with a water-based lubricating jelly or antibiotic ointment and using a bulb syringe to create gentle suction and provide massage, as described above, to mobilize the egg(s). If these procedures don't result in relieving the impaction, a veterinarian should be consulted since surgery may be needed. The snake should be observed closely for complications from stress, hydrated well, allowed to eat if it chooses, and given privacy and common sense care.

OTHER HEALTH PROBLEMS

Obesity: Obesity, or excessive fat deposits, is caused by overfeeding. A zealous keeper who deliberately overfeeds his snake in order to increase growth is courting disaster. Each snake has very specific metabolic needs, and if the food eaten is more than what the metabolism demands, the excess is stored as fat in the muscle and connective tissues as well as in the liver and circulatory system. The excessive weight of an obese snake will slow it down, which is contrary to what it needs; activity is very important in helping to burn calories. Other problems that develop include added stress on the lungs and heart due to fat deposits, and improper chemical balances due to interference with digestive processes.

Look at it from another point of view: A keeper who overfeeds his juvenile Burmese Python, *P. molurus bivittatus*, in order to make sure it's the same size as a breeding adult by the time it's 12 months old is not going to have a sexually mature adult at 12 months, just a very large juvenile.

Most boas and pythons like to eat, but the keeper must keep this in moderation or their pets will suffer from extreme obesity. Photo of D'Albert's Python.

Captive Breeding Information

MATING

In captivity, the usual time that mating activity occurs may or may not be the same as when it takes place in the wild. Many factors will determine what time of year the snakes will mate, such as geographical location while in captivity, photoperiod manipulation, environmental humidity, temperature fluctuations (often used to induce breeding), and general husbandry practices.

Temperature fluctuations are probably the most important aspect to be manipulated to induce breeding and promote fertility. All snakes require some degree of cooling prior to mating, usually for at least four weeks, but occasionally a little longer. Separation of the pair is recommended since the males should be cooled with slightly lower temperatures. Care must be taken to monitor the individual's response to cooling by looking for loss of appetite, poor color, unusual irritability, or lethargy.

Mating should occur after the temperature of the environment is gradually raised over a seven-day period, humidity is increased by direct misting of lukewarm water,

A pair of Rough-scaled Sand Boas, *Eryx conicus*, entwined during copulation. Photo by Jim Merli.

Facing Page: A hatching Burmese Python, *Python molurus bivittatus*. Photo by B. Kahl.

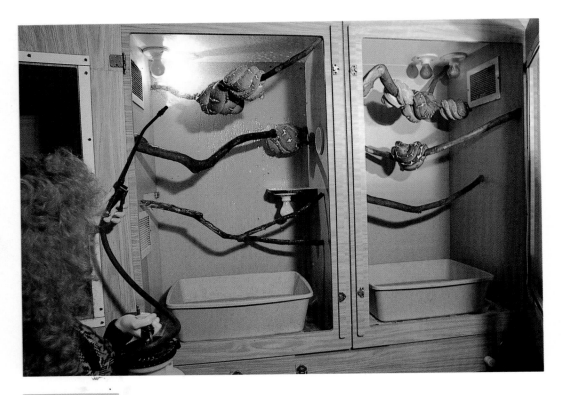

and all other requirements of individual species are honored. For example, our specimens of *Chondropython viridis* have a tendency to mate during only the night hours regardless of photoperiod manipulation. Best results are obtained by using a three- to five-day trial period, then separating the pair as before, except maintaining the warmer temperature. This sequence should be repeated during the entire mating process.

Best results are obtained by placing the female into the male's environment, since males are dominant. Hiding and burrowing requirements for certain species also must be met while still providing for observation of the pair. For example, a regular shoebox placed so that viewing can take place through an opening in one end, while still assuring privacy, works well.

Other ways to induce mating include feeding specimens on a regular basis, keeping environments clean and sanitized, and providing for the overall health of the specimens. Supplements of vitamin D3 in the diet and the use of a full-spectrum ultraviolet light source are both essential requirements for breeding specimens in captivity and increasing fertility.

Note: Always be sure specimens are properly sexed as pairs, since placing two males together could cause injury while still appearing similar to mating activity.

GESTATION AND INCUBATION

How do you tell if your snake is gravid?

Most persons would agree that this is probably one of the most complicated aspects of breeding snakes in captivity. The following are several suggestions. The first and most obvious is increasing body girth. This is demonstrated by expansion of the spaces between the scales along the lateral and ventral sides of the body. Be aware that increased girth also can occur during ovulation prior to actual fertilization. Other signs of pregnancy include changes in behavior, such as increased or decreased activity; irritability; searching for an appropriate nesting spot; and in some cases, extreme adversity toward the male when placed together. Gravid females may fast or may have increased appetites while they are in the gestation process. Each individual

Unlike the eggs of most herptiles, python eggs can be very large—some even larger than those of various farm fowl. Photo of Burmese Python, *Python molurus bivittatus*, eggs by Jim Merli.

may react differently to being in a gravid state, so there is no way to be completely sure until offspring or eggs are produced.

Approximately one week before egg laying or live birth occurs, the female will shed. When labor commences, it is absolutely essential that sterile nesting materials be available. Vermiculite and sphagnum moss make good substrates for live birth, laying eggs, and incubation material. Miscarriages and/or infertile eggs often occur if the snake is stressed due to improper handling, feeding, temperature, or overall environmental conditions.

Python eggs are white and may be uniformly round, oval, or even oblong, depending on the species. An infertile egg may be smaller than usual, mottled yellowish tan and creamy in color, and may feel oily to the touch. If there is any doubt as to the fertility of the eggs, they should be incubated as usual and monitored closely. Frequently fertile eggs will be laid in clusters and adhere together. Such eggs should not be separated, as damage could result to the developing embryo.

Some breeders prefer to allow the female python to naturally incubate the eggs herself. She will

Due to the great progress of today's captive breeding efforts, unique specimens like this striking albino Boa Constrictor, *Boa constrictor*, are now being seen for the first time. Photo by W. P. Mara.

proceed to coil around the egg pile and may seem to be having spasms. These are an attempt to increase her body temperature. Self-incubation may not be the method of choice for the following reasons: hatching ratios are frequently less, it is more difficult to manipulate environmental factors such as temperature and humidity since essentially there are two separate requirements that must be met (one for the female and one for the eggs), and due to the lack of movement of the female, bacterial diseases and open lesions can occur and possibly affect the health of the incubating snake as well as the eggs.

Artificial incubation is preferred by many breeders. There are several ways to accomplish this. A still-air incubator that can be purchased or made out of household materials works best. Most purchased incubators include a thermostat and a receptacle that is filled with water that heats and humidifies the surrounding air without allowing the eggs to become wet. To make a homemade incubator, provide a low heat source under and/or around an

Occasionally pythons will display a trait that is very unusual for snakes—they will incubate their own eggs. Photo of *Liasis perthensis* by R. T. Hoser.

incubator made out of any plastic receptacle or glass aquarium, with a cover or cellophane wrapping to keep the humidity inside. Vermiculite and sphagnum moss, moistened slightly so that you can knead them in your hands, make good substrates in both kinds of incubators. Be sure that all electrical work is safe— you are dealing with resistance coils to produce heat,   and these may melt or damage many everyday materials.

Never allow the substrate or eggs to get wet! When removing eggs from the original environment, they should be cupped in the palm of your hand along with the substrate material in which they were laid and very gently placed in the incubator, resting on top of the substrate. Do not turn them either; they should remain in the exact position in which they were laid.

Eggs may become indented due to lack of moisture in the surrounding air and may look spoiled but in fact be fine. A way to solve this problem is to indent the substrate with your finger and place the eggs into the depression, covering all but the tops so they can

breathe. The moisture in the substrate will provide increased humidity and be absorbed by the egg. Again, make sure the substrate is not wet, and never spray the actual egg.

In some cases, fully developed embryos can go a full term of incubation and fail to hatch. This can occur for several reasons: stress due to frequent viewing and/or handling, excessive light, or premature opening of the eggs by the breeder. Making a small slit-like opening in the top of the eggs is a practice used by many breeders and often is successful in assisting the neonates out of the

This stunning photograph shows the newborn of a viviparous species (in this case the Cuban Boa, *Epicrates angulifer*) breaking through what is known as the egg membrane. Photo by K. H. Switak.

eggs. Usually this is not necessary since healthy neonates are well-equipped to do the job themselves.

Although more attention has been given to the egg-laying snakes, live-bearers need similar kinds of care. Here, of course, the embryos are being incubated inside the female. Humidity needs can be provided by spraying the female as well as the substrate with small amounts of warm water two to three times daily. Temperature needs can be met by red heat lamps on low settings and space

heaters to increase the general room temperature. Spot heating items such as heat rocks and heating pads are not recommended during gestation; due to the lack of movement by the female, blisters or burns can occur.

NEONATAL CARE

Neonates emerge in an embryonic sac that they break out of within one hour. In some cases, the sac may appear to be dry and the neonate appears dead. This may not be the case, however, and an attempt should be made to revive the newborn. For example, this was accomplished with a specimen of the Mexican Rosy Boa, *Lichanura trivirgata trivirgata*, by placing the neonate, including the embryonic sac, into a shallow warm water bath for 30 to 60 minutes, resulting in the revival of the neonate, which survived. If neonates of any kind have trouble coming out of their eggs or embryonic sacs, the best way to assist them is to increase the humidity and let them do it naturally rather than manually remove them. The safety of the animal is the most important factor. There is no need to remove the umbilical cord, as it will dry and fall off on its own.

The next major undertaking is meeting the requirements of the neonates, which can be very time-consuming. Feeding of neonates should be attempted two to three days after they shed their first skin. Within that first week or so they are being nourished by the yolk they absorbed prior to birth. They do require

Some newborn boas and pythons will resemble their parents in every way, whereas others will boast what is often called a "juvenile pattern" that changes as the snake grows. Photo of a juvenile "red phase" Garden Tree Boa, *Corallus enydris enydris*, by R. D. Bartlett.

This young Ringed Python, *Liasis boa*, may have orange markings right now, but as it grows and matures that color will become a dull brown. Photo by Paul Freed.

water, however, but be absolutely sure it is in a shallow dish and no more than one inch deep because neonates can and will drown. The requirements provided for adults usually work well with neonates too, except remember that they are babies and can injure themselves out of

depending on the size of the neonate. Occasionally, though, they will accept only specific food items, and it's this point that often requires a "green thumb" to determine exactly how to get them to eat. For example, neonates of the Emerald Tree Boa, *Corallus caninus*, and the Green Tree Boa,

ignorance. For example, spot heaters such as hot rocks can cause severe injury if a neonate sits on it continually, which is a common occurrence.

Neonates usually will accept pre-killed pink mice and rats as initial foods, sized appropriately

Chondropython viridis, often will accept only pink mice that have been rubbed with chicken entrails. Rubbing the pink mice or rats with other animal material such as lizards or birds will stimulate the snakes's appetites and let them become familiar with the taste of rodents. Live rodents sometimes are preferred by neonates,

HIBERNATION

Whether or not to "hibernate" your snake is a very controversial subject

which eventually should be substituted with pre-killed foods. Force-feeding should be a last resort, but may become necessary if refusal to eat becomes prolonged. Meeting the general requirements of the environment, especially cleanliness and privacy, usually will improve the neonates' willingness to eat. Force-feeding should only be attempted by professionals experienced in the proper methods since injury and death may result even with professional handling.

that many keepers of boas and pythons inquire about. In the wild, snakes are affected by seasonal changes in temperature and humidity, such as during monsoon or rainy seasons (in some parts of the world). Usually temperatures will be lower or daylight hours shorter in the "winter" months. Again, it all depends on the part of the world they come from. Mating usually takes place just after the temperatures begin to rise ("spring") and frequently during rainy seasons.

Although sexually immature young cannot breed, many keepers still prefer to give them some sort of hibernation-type rest period. This must be done with extreme care. Photo of a juvenile Madagascan Tree Boa, *Sanzinia madagascariensis*, by Paul Freed.

Because snakes are cold-blooded, meaning they obtain warmth from their environment guess what happens when the weather is cold? Their metabolism slows down, they become less active, and they "hibernate." This is a normal process, and one that has been determined to be a benefit to the snakes, especially in a controlled situation. The snake is allowed to take a rest from eating and other activities that take energy and devote some time to low-energy activities such as developing oocytes and sperm (reproductive cells). Many snakes will have periods when they won't eat and will be inactive despite the keeper's attempts to induce the opposite. In this situation the snake is attempting to hibernate (unless of course it is sick), and the temperature should be lowered to accommodate this need, particularly if the snake isn't eating. If it is malnourished, hibernation is not a good idea until the snake eats several times. Wild-caught snakes in particular are apt to hibernate on their own schedule, which, depending on where they originated, may be quite different from the native snakes in your area of the world. Captive-born specimens will hibernate when deliberately cooled, and this can be manipulated by alterations in temperature as well as lighting. Temperatures need to be cooled gradually over a two-week period (about five degrees per week), and the light provided during the day shortened, so that the snake experiences a day that has more night hours with cooler temperatures to mimic fall and winter seasons. Keep in mind that the temperature is affected by central heating; attempts made to warm the keeper can also warm the snake.

Air conditioners of course can affect the temperature during the summer, the environment actually being cooler in the summer than in the winter. If the snake is housed by the window, it will be affected by the day/night durations of the outside environment as well as by the humidity levels when it rains. Sounds complicated? It is, but it's necessary too, especially if you intend to breed your snakes. Reproductive cells are destroyed by excessive heat, which may have a big role in infertility problems.

Popular Species

The following brief accounts of some of the more popular and commonly bred boas and pythons are intended to provide the beginning breeder with essential information for successful breeding and care of the young.

DUMERIL'S BOA
(ACRANTOPHIS DUMERILI)

This pretty brown and tan serpent hails from the rainforests of Madagascar and Reunion and sometimes grows to a length of over 10 feet. The pairs mate from October to January. After a remarkable 200- to 250-day gestation period, the mother gives birth to between seven and 15 reasonably large (16 to 18 inches) young.

If you're breeding Dumeril's Boa in captivity, it's best to keep the males slightly cooler than the females (70 to 75°F as opposed to 80 to 82° F); remember to leave the two in complete privacy during copulation.

When the young are born, maintain them at a comfortable 80° F and use small, fuzzy mice as the food source.

MADAGASCAN GROUND BOA
(ACRANTOPHIS MADAGASCARIENSIS)

Of the two *Acrantophis*, this one is the larger. Measuring in at over 12

Not often seen in the hobby but nevertheless an attractive and hardy captive, Dumeril's Boa, *Acrantophis dumerili*, is native to the rainforest regions of Reunion and Madagascar. Photo by Ken Lucas, Steinhart Aquarium.

feet, even the young can stretch beyond two feet.

In captivity, breeeding *madagascariensis* is a virtual breeze. Their ideal reproductive period lasts from August to December. The pair should be kept separate until that time and at slightly different temperatures (males: 70 to 75°F; females: 80 to 85°F).

The young, which are born in a litter of between two and six, also will need to be kept at a consistent 82° F and should be fed small mice. in the pet trade, *A. madagascariensis* only appears every now and again. It commands a fairly high price.

THE COMMON (AND RED-TAILED)
BOA CONSTRICTOR
(BOA CONSTRICTOR)

One of the most popular and widely seen snakes in the pet industry, the Common Boa and all its many subspecies make fine breeding stock. Native to the warmth of Mexico, Central and South America, and the Lesser Antilles, the adults will require about 80°F to breed. The female, while being kept at a high 82 to 85° F before actual copulation begins (as opposed to the male at 70°F), will gestate for a period of about 150 to 250 days before giving birth to a litter of anywhere from eight to 60 respectable-sized young (14" to 20"). These neonates should be fed young pre-killed mice, and care should be taken not to place them in tanks with too many wood products (shavings, etc.).

THE PACIFIC BOA (OR VIPER BOA)
(CANDOIA CARINATA)

From New Guinea and the Solomon and Tokelau Islands comes the Pacific Boa, a relatively small boid (only up to 4 feet) that mates from March through May.

During the captive breeding process, the female should be warmed

The Boa Constrictor, *Boa constrictor*, has probably enjoyed the longest-running commercial popularity of all the boids. And rightly so—it is an excellent captive. Photo by B. Kahl.

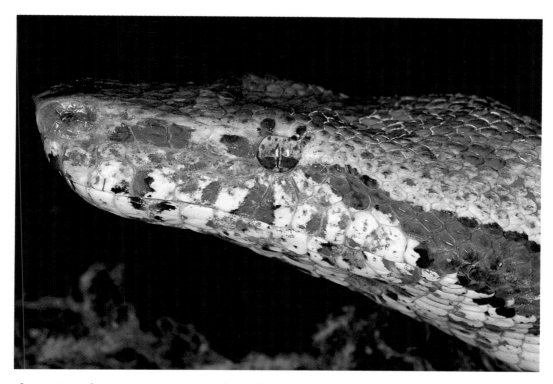

about ten degrees more than the male (at around 80°F), and then raised another five degrees when gravid. After a 150- to 200-day gestation period, she will give birth to from five to 20 young that will measure anywhere from 6 inches to one foot in length. They should be kept in a quiet, warm container with plenty of room to hide, and sustained on a diet of small mice. The other members of this genus can be bred the same way.

RUBBER BOA
(CHARINA BOTTAE)

One of only two boa species native to the United States, this handsome 3-foot snake mates from February to May. The females have a gestation period of 100 to 150 days, and the mother will then give birth to a litter of between two and six small young (five to 10 inches).

Captive care for the newborns is basically the same as it is for the adults: some soft substrate for burrowing, a cool, quiet hide, and of course the essential water bowl, rock, etc. They will feed on both small birds and mice, but the latter is obviously preferable.

EMERALD TREE BOA
(CORALLUS CANINUS)

A very popular pet

One of the smaller boids is this sub-species of the Pacific Island Boa, *Candoia carinata paulsoni*, rarely growing over 4 feet. Photo by K. H. Switak.

Facing Page: On the top is a bizarre pattern mutation of Boa Constrictor; on the bottom is a normal specimen. Photos by John Coborn and Roberta Kayne, respectively.

The Rubber Boa, *Charina bottae*, is one of only two boid species native to the United States. Photo by K. H. Switak.

species, although somewhat expensive, the Emerald Tree Boa is fairly easy to breed in captivity. Being native to northern South America, it naturally requires very warm surroundings in order to procreate. The males should be kept slightly cooler than the females before breeding actually begins (about 70 to 75°F vs 80°F) and then introduced into warmer surroundings when copulation begins. The mother will have a gestation period of about 200 to 250 days, at the end of which she will produce a live litter of about two to 15 neonates. They will measure anywhere from 16 to 19 inches, and should be fed lizards or small mice. Keep them in a tall, moist, warm terrarium with a few branches since they are highly arboreal.

GARDEN TREE BOA
(CORALLUS ENYDRIS ENYDRIS)

This South American boid ranges in size from 48 inches to 72 inches (12 inches to 16 inches for the young). Its usual time of mating is from December to March, and the mother's gestation time is about 200 days (150–250).

If you are planning on breeding them in captivity, it is best to keep the male at about 70–75° F beforehand (female about five to ten degrees higher) and then introduce the pair in the male's cage at about 80°F.

The size of an average

Only now are hobbyists beginning to keep and breed the Garden Tree Boa, *Corallus enydris*. Photo of a juvenile specimen by W. P. Mara.

The genus *Corallus* has provided the hobby with many fine snake species, but the most popular overall is probably the Emerald Tree Boa, *Corallus caninus*. Photo of an orange young specimen by S. Kochetov.

The Garden Tree Boa, *Corallus enydris*, is almost exclusively arboreal, so keepers should provide one with as many branches as possible. Photo by B. Kahl.

litter of young is about three to 15. These should be fed either chicks, mice, or small lizards. They are best kept in a moderate-size terrarium and given frequent mistings and a few branches to climb on much like the adults.

CUBAN BOA
(EPICRATES ANGULIFER)

The Cuban Boa is, needless to say, native to Cuba, and attains a length of about 10 feet. They mate from March through May in their native habitat, and the neonates are born at a length of about 15 inches. These young will take small birds and mice, but the latter is obviously preferable.

When keeping them in captivity, it is best to give the adults plenty of room, and keep them, as well as the young, at a temperature of about 80°F

Since *Corallus* species occur in warmer regions, daily mistings to maintain the humidity levels are advised. Photo by S. Kochetov.

Cuban Boas, *Epicrates angulifer*, are not seen in the hobby too often. Perhaps it is their preference for birds that accounts for this. Photo by S. Kochetov.

A very popular hobby snake is the Rainbow Boa, *Epicrates cenchria*. It responds well to captive surroundings and breeds without much fuss. Photo by K. T. Nemuras.

(less for the males right before breeding). It also is a wise idea to provide some form of hiding space as well as a few branches, since they like to climb.

THE RAINBOW BOA
(EPICRATES CENCHRIA)

This mid-sized South American serpent (48 to 60 inches) mates in early spring and has a litter size of eight to 15. If you are breeding them in captivity, remember to keep the males slightly cooler than the females beforehand (68 to 75°F, as opposed to 80°F), and then give them both at least 80°F during copulation. The young will be about a foot to a foot and a half in length and should be fed pinkie mice or chicks regularly.

Finally, *cenchria* should have a secure hiding place and a few branches to climb on.

PUERTO RICAN BOA
(EPICRATES INORNATUS)

Neonates of this species are about 12 to 15 inches in length. Although their environmental requirements are basically the same as their parents' (80°F), special attention should be given to giving these little serpents a few branches since they like to climb.

The adults will breed from March to May, and the males should be kept at about 70 to 75°F beforehand, the females being about ten degrees higher. When the young are born, feed them young fuzzy mice or, if you can supply them, even some small birds.

HAITIAN BOA
(EPICRATES STRIATUS)

This pretty animal has a range extending over Hispaniola to the Bahamas. The average adult size is quite impressive: 72 to 96 inches, and the neonates are quite respectable as well, being from 16 to 20 inches.

They mate from December to May, with the female having a gestation period of about 200 days (150 to 250). Before breeding them,

Litter size for the Rainbow Boa, *Epicrates cenchria*, usually ranges somewhere around one dozen. These young will be about one foot long and should take pinkie mice right away. Photo by Jim Merli.

This subspecies of the Rainbow Boa, *Epicrates cenchria alvarezi*, is not as common in the herp hobby as *E. c. cenchria*, but would still do just as well. Photo by Jim Merli.

cool the male down to about 70 to 75° F and raise the female up from 80 to 85°F.

When the young are born give them pinkie mice if possible, but don't be surprised if all you can get them to eat are lizards.

JAMAICAN BOA
(EPICRATES SUBFLAVUS)

The Jamaican Boa will mate from December through May and the female will have a gestation period of between 200 and 250 days. As with most other boas and pythons, the male should be cooled about ten degrees lower

than the female prior to the mate (at about 70°F) and then copulation can begin.

The young, which will be about 10 to 15 inches in length, should be fed pinkie mice or lizards and be given plenty of room and privacy, as should the adults. The usual litter size will be from 10 to 30. They should be kept at about 80°F.

This species is endangered.

EGYPTIAN SAND BOA
(ERYX COLUBRINUS)

Before breeding this species you should always make sure the adults have three things: plenty of

The Virgin Islands Tree Boa, *Epicrates monensis granti*, is one of the rarer boids—the only place you'll see its name is on endangered lists. Photo by Roberta Kayne.

The more "common" *E. monensis* subspecies is the nominate race, *Epicrates monensis monensis*. This animal was first described in 1898. Photo by Roberta Kayne.

space, warm surroundings, and at least two weeks of "climatic preparation." This means the males should be kept at about 70 to 74°F and the females at least 80° F.

When the young are born, in a litter of four to 20, they will be about six to ten inches in length (the adults are not much larger—15 to 30 inches) and can survive on a diet of small lizards or young mice. They will need some soft substrate in which to burrow, as will the females, and about 80°F for their cage temperature.

INDIAN SAND BOA
(ERYX JOHNII)

The usual time of mating for this snake is from April to August. The gestation period for the females is rather short, comparatively speaking, at 100 to 160 days, and they should be kept about 10 to 15 degrees warmer than the males prior to copulation, at around 80 to 85°F.

The young, which will be about 6 to 10 inches long at birth, will require plenty of burrowing material, a secure hiding place, and a large shallow water bowl that gets cleaned and re-filled daily. They should be fed pinkie mice or lizards.

The Green Anaconda, *Eunectes murinus*, holds a place of high regard in the serpent kingdom—it is one of the longest snakes in the world. Specimens have been known to grow over 28 feet. Photo by B. Kahl.

GREEN ANACONDA
(EUNECTES MURINUS)

This is one of the largest snakes in the world. It can attain an adult length of well over 25 feet , and even the young can be born very close to three.

A native of South America, the Green Anaconda mates from March until May, and the females will gestate for 200 to 250 days. If you are breeding them in captivity, it might be a good idea to cool the males down to about 70° to 75°F before

on a diet of mice and rats; same with the young.

YELLOW ANACONDA
(EUNECTES NOTAEUS)

This South American snake mates from Ocotber to December, with the females having a gestation period of 200 to 250 days. Cool the males before breeding them (70 to 75°F) and give the pair a large enclosure at about 80 to 85°F.

When the young are born they should measure about 20 to 25 inches (the adults attain only a length of about 12 feet), and should be fed mice, birds, or pinkie rats. The average litter size can range anywhere from five to 25.

ROSY BOA
(LICHANURA TRIVIRGATA)

This is one of only two boas found in the United States. It is native to California, Arizona, and Baja Mexico. The average adult size is only 2 to 3 feet, which is somewhat small for a boa. The young are only 8 to 12 inches when born.

They mate from March through June, with the males and females being reasonably close in temperature beforehand (75°F vs. 80°F). The gestation period will last for about 175 days, at the end of which time a litter

copulation. Then, when the female becomes gravid, give her a temperature of about 85°F until she gives birth.

A large enclosure is the best bet since these serpents obviously get very large, and they can subsist

At one time, neither of the United States boid species was common to the herp hobby. Now, Rosy Boas, *Lichanura trivirgata*, have become favorites. Photo by Isabelle Francais.

of only two to five young will be born. These young should be fed pinkie mice and kept at a temperature of about 80°F, as should the adults.

MADAGASCAN TREE BOA
(SANZINIA MADAGASCARIENSIS)

A native of Madagascar, this relatively small boa (48 to 72 inches) mates from December to May.

The females have a gestation period of 150 to 250 days and should be kept warm before actual copulation begins (80 to 85°F, ten degrees less for the males).

When the young are born, they will measure in at about one and a half feet and should be fed small rodents and birds. The average litter size is anywhere from five to 15.

The babies should be kept warm (80°F), with a few branches for climbing.

This is an endangered species.

BIMINI DWARF BOA
(TROPIDOPHIS CANUS CURTUS)

Hailing from the beautiful Bahamas, this 2- to 3-foot boa (only 4 to 6 inches for the young) mates from December to May, with the female gestation period being from 110 to 150 days. If you are breeding them in captivity, it would be best to cool the males down before actual copulation (70 to 75°F) and raise the females up slightly (80 to 85°F).

When the young are born, it would be best to feed them small lizards, frogs, or, preferably, very small rodents, and keep them housed in a large container with plenty of burrowing material. They are primarily nocturnal.

Note the unusual color pattern on this young Madagascan Tree Boa, *S. madagascar- iensis.* Although attractive, the design will change with age. Photo by R. D. Bartlett.

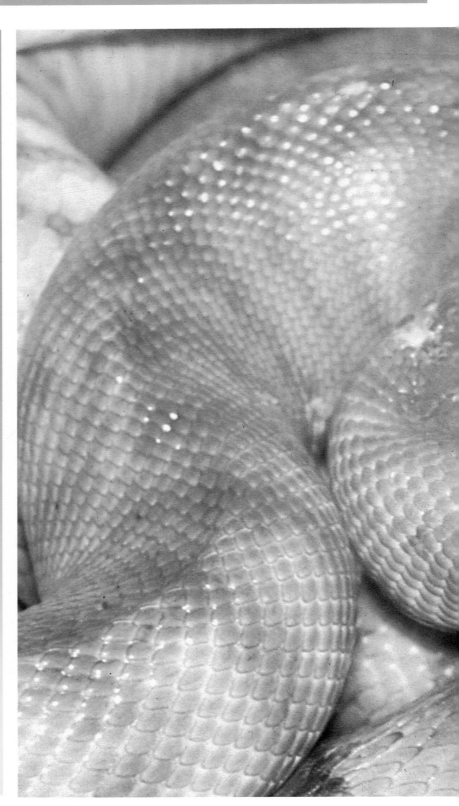

The stunning Ramsay's Python, *Aspidites ramsayi*, is a native of the drier regions of southern Australia and an excellent, mild-tempered captive. Photo by R. T. Hoser.

CENTRAL AMERICAN DWARF BOA
(UNGALIOPHIS PANAMENSIS)

Ranging from western Colombia to southern Nicaragua, this tiny boa (20 to 30 inches) usually mates during the winter months. The normal gestation period for the females is believed to be around 150 days, and the average litter size is between 10 to 20. The young are quite small, 6 inches or so.

When keeping them in captivity, remember to always cool the males before mating them (75°F for females, 80 to 85°F for females). Make sure they are kept warm the rest of the time (80°F). Provide plenty of branches to climb on.

This is a somewhat rare species and seldom seen in captivity.

BLACK-HEADED PYTHON
(ASPIDITES MELANOCEPHALUS)

A native of both the non-arid and arid regions of northern Australia, this snake attains a length of over 90 inches (12 to 15 inches in the neonates). Its usual time of mating is from December to February, and the female's gestation period will last a little over 100 days. Before breeding, you should cool the males to about 70 to 75°F and keep the females a bit higher at 80°F. Other requirements include ample hiding and nesting spots and a consistent, well-rounded diet.

The average number of eggs in a clutch can range from six to 12. The incubation of the eggs should last around 60 to 80 days. The incubation temperature should be rather high, from 85 to 90°F, with the humidity being about 80 to 100%. The young will have a very high metabolism and should be fed pinkie mice regularly.

RAMSAY'S PYTHON
(ASPIDITES RAMSAYI)

From the arid regions of Australia comes Ramsay's Python, which can grow to a length of about 7 feet. It mates from December to February and will take about 100 to 120 days before the eggs are laid. If you're breeding them in captivity, remember to

One of the more attractive and yet lesser-seen members of the boid family is the Black-headed Python, *Aspidites melanocephalus*. They are reportedly easy to breed as well. Photo by R. D. Bartlett.

Facing Page: Two views of the Calabar Burrowing Python, *Calabaria reinhardtii.* On top, the defensive posture (with tail obvious and head tucked in), and beneath, a closeup of the head. Photos by Jim Merli and P. J. Stafford, respectively.

keep the males cooler than the females beforehand (75°F vs. 85°F).

An average clutch is about six to 12 eggs that should hatch out in about 60 to 80 days. The artificial incubation process requires a temperature of about 85°F and a humidity level of about 90%. The young will measure around one foot and should be fed pinkie mice or lizards on a very regular basis.

RINGED PYTHON
(LIASIS BOA)

Found in the Bismarck Archipelago, this beautiful and rare python grows to a length of over 7 feet (the young are 8 to 10 inches long). They will mate from December to March, and a gestation time of about 140 days then follows. The females will lay six to 12 smooth white eggs that will hatch in anywhere from 60 to 80 days. Incubate them at 85°F with a humidity level of over 80%.

If you are planning to breed these pythons in captivity, make sure the males are kept cooler than the females beforehand (70 to 75°F vs. 80 to 85°F) and then mate them at 80°F. Their tanks should have adequate hiding spots and a humidity level of about 70%. Feed the young pinkie mice.

CALABAR PYTHON
(CALABARIA REINHARDTII)

This species is found only in West Africa and attains a length of about 3 feet. The young are already a foot long at birth.

Their usual time of mating is from December to May, and the egg-development process usually lasts for about 100 to 120 days. Keep the pair, and the young as well, in thickly-bedded, humid tanks (about 70%) with a temperature of around 80°F.

When incubating the eggs (average clutch size around five), be sure to keep the temperature at no less than 82 to 85°F and the humidity level at about 80 to 100%. The newborn's first food should be rodents.

GREEN TREE PYTHON
(CHONDROPYTHON VIRIDIS)

Relatively speaking, this is a reasonably small python (adults: 48 to 72 inches, young: up to one foot). It hails from Australia and New Guinea and breeds from January to March and also from July to September.

This species has an average clutch of about ten to 25 eggs. The normal gestation period for a healthy female is around 115 days, and the normal

incubation time is about 40 to 60 days.

If you are planning on breeding the Green Tree Python it is a good idea to cool the males down slightly beforehand (at about 70°F) and make sure the females have a nesting box. The eggs should be incubated at about 85 to 90°F with a humidity level of about 80 to 100%. The young should be given pinkie mice for their first meal.

D'ALBERT'S PYTHON
(LIASIS ALBERTISII)

A native of Australia, New Guinea, and the Islands of the Torres Straits, this large serpent (72 to 96 inches) breeds from June to November.

When mating them in captivity, be sure to cool the males down to about 70°F first. Give the pair a warm, humid cage, and give the female a nesting box. She will lay her eggs usually about 100 to 130 days after the breeding. The eggs, the clutch size of which is from eight to 20, should hatch in 60 to 80 days. The young should be about a foot in length and will take pinkie mice and lizards.

Artificial incubation requires a temperature of about 85 to 90°F and a humidity level of over 80%.

The Green Tree Python, *Chondropython viridis*, will not be born with any hint of emerald green coloring, but rather a reddish orange, then change to yellow in sub-adulthood (shown here), and finally the brilliant green for which it is so well known. Photo by B. Kahl.

CHILDREN'S PYTHON
(LIASIS CHILDRENI)

A native of northern Australia, this snake is quite small (only up to 48 inches).

They mate from December to February, and after a 100- to 150-day development period the female lays a clutch of three to 15 eggs. These will hatch in about 40 to 80 days. The young will measure just over 6 inches.

If you are artificially incubating the eggs, be sure to give them a high temperature (85°F) and a humidity of at least 80%. The young will take mice and lizards, but obviously the former and preferable.

BROWN WATER PYTHON
(LIASIS FUSCUS)

The Brown Water Python is quite a good-sized snake (72 to 96 inches) that hails from northeastern Australia and New Guinea. The young usually do not measure over one foot.

When breeding them in captivity be sure to cool the males down to about 70°F beforehand and then give the pair plenty of room and high humidity at 80 to 85°F. The female will develop her eggs internally for about 110 days and then lay a clutch of seven to 15 that should hatch 40 to 60 days. During artificial incubation it is best to keep the humidity high (80%) and the temperature at least 82°F.

The neonates should be maintained on a diet of pinkie mice.

MACKLOT'S PYTHON
(LIASIS MACKLOTI)

Macklot's Python can attain a length of up to 96 inches and hails from New Guinea. It mates from December through May, and the time from mating until actual egg-laying occurs is about 100 to 120

The Children's Python, *Liasis childreni*, has only recently been seen as a reliable hobby species. It is one of the most abundant boids in Australia. Photo by C. Banks.

Facing Page: Two views of D'Albert's Python Top: black adult male. Bottom: Head of adult female. Photos by W. P. Mara and courtesy of the Chester Zoo, respectively.

days. Before breeding them in captivity, be sure the males are cooled to about 70°F beforehand. When copulation begins, be sure to provide at least a 60% humidty level.

The average egg clutch this female will produce should number around seven to 15. If incubated properly (85 to 90°F, 80% humidity), they should hatch in anywhere from 40 to 60 days. The young will measure just under one foot and should be fed pinkie mice.

OLIVE PYTHON
(LIASIS OLIVACEUS)

A native of northern Australia, this python is a December to March breeder measuring in at about 80 to 85 inches (6 to 10 inches for the young). It takes about 100 to 120 days for the female to lay her eggs (a clutch of around 10 to 25). These should be incubated at a temperature of about 85°F with a humidity level not less than 80%.

The adults require plenty of room, so should be given a large tank and a soft substrate. The humidity here should be high as well. Don't forget to cool the males down before breeding them (70°F).

When the young are born, try to start them on a diet of pinkie mice.

PYGMY PYTHON
(LIASIS PERTHENSIS)

This western Australian native, also known as the Ant-hill Python, is relatively small, the adults almost never reaching over 3 feet. They are born only slightly over 6 inches long.

They will breed from December to March. The female will gestate for about 100 to 120 days before finally laying a clutch of two to five large white eggs. Be sure to cool the males down to about 70°F before introducing the female.

Care for the eggs includes a humidity level of over 80% and a temperature of no less than 85°F. The neonates will require water, a soft substrate, and a diet of, preferably, young mice, although small lizards might be sought.

The Pygmy Python is a somewhat rare species and almost never seen in captivity.

STIMSON DESERT PYTHON
(LIASIS STIMSONI)

Found only in Central Australia, this relatively small (24") python breeds from December to March and has a gestation period of anywhere from 120 to 150 days. If you are planning on breeding them in captivity, be sure to provide the pair with

Bredl's Python, *Morelia bredli*, was only described in 1981, but has already become a hobby sensation. Photo by C. Banks.

plenty of burrowing and hiding material and make sure the males are cooled down to about 70°F beforehand.

The average egg clutch for this species is reasonably small, about two to five, but the eggs themselves are somewhat large. The incubation period lasts from 40 to 60 days and should be done with about an 80% humidity at about 85°F. The young will measure about half a foot.

BREDL'S PYTHON
(MORELIA BREDLI)

These pythons mate in the wild from December to February, the female laying her eggs about 125

Regardless of their sometimes outrageous price, Bredl's Pythons, *Morelia bredli*, are still in very high demand. Photo by C. Banks.

The Diamond Python, *Morelia spilotes spilotes*, grows to a length of about 10 feet and is very attractive, but captives reportedly do not do well. Photo by C. Banks.

days later. When breeding them in captivity, make sure the males are cooled beforehand (70°F) and give the pair plenty of hiding space and privacy.

The average number of eggs in a Bredl's litter is about five (three to eight). The incubation period, which should be carried out at an 80% humidity and at least 85°F, lasts around 40 to 60 days. The young, which will be about 8 to 10 inches long (adults 65 inches), should be given pinkie mice for their diet.

NORTHERN ROCK PYTHON
(MORELIA CARINATUS)

A native of the northwestern region in Australia, the adults of this species attain a length of about 6 feet (just under one foot in the young). They mate from December until February. If you're planning on breeding them in captivity, don't forget to cool the males down to about 70°F beforehand.

An average clutch size for the species numbers around nine, and the incubation period lasts about 40 to 60 days. When incubating them domestically be sure to provide a temperature of at least 85°F and a humidity level of over 80%. The young should be fed pinkie mice or, less preferably, lizards.

This python is extremely rare and almost never seen in collections.

DIAMOND PYTHON
(MORELIA SPILOTES SPILOTES)

Found in New South Wales and coastal eastern Australia, the Diamond

Python breeds from December through February after a brief "hibernation" period at about 70°F. The adults grow to just under 8 feet, and the young just over one.

The normal gestation time for the females is roughly 135 days, at the end of which about one dozen eggs will be laid. These eggs, if incubated properly at at least 85°F with an 80% humidity, should hatch in about 40 to 60 days. Give the young pinkie mice as a first meal and make sure their tanks are misted frequently.

CARPET PYTHON
(MORELIA SPILOTES VARIEGATUS)

This Australian snake (actually a subspecies of the Diamond Python) is fairly good-sized: some of the adults can grow to almost 10 feet! The young usually are over 2 feet right from the egg. If you do decide to breed the Carpet Python, make sure the males have been kept at about 70°F beforehand or they will not be able to fertilize the eggs properly. The best time to mate them is from December to February. A normal gestation period lasts about 135 days (110 to 150).

The average number of eggs in a clutch should be anywhere from seven to 15. With the proper conditions (85°F and 80% humidity), these should hatch in about 50 days. Feed the young pinkie mice.

This Carpet Python comes in a wide variety of beautiful color patterns.

AMETHYSTINE PYTHON
(PYTHON AMETHYSTINUS)

One of the largest serpents in the world, this native of Australia and New Guinea sometimes attains a length of well over 23 feet! When you consider that the young are only one and a half feet in length at birth, that fact becomes even more intriguing.

If you are actually in possession of two of these monsters and decide you might like to try breeding them, don't forget to cool the male down beforehand. Females have a gestation period of about 135 days, after which time 10 to 25 eggs will be laid. Incubate these at a temperature of over 85°F with a humidity level not less than 80%.

The neonates should be given a few tree branches, as they will spend some time off the ground, and a shallow but large water bowl, for both bathing and drinking. Feed them small rodents.

A New Guinea snake, Boelen's Python, *Python boeleni*, is an even-tempered creature that makes a good captive although it is not often available. Photo by Jim Merli.

Facing Page: Two of the less often seen members of the genus *Python*. On the top, Boelen's Python, *Python boeleni*; on the bottom, the Angolan Python, *Python anchietae*. Photos by Jim Merli and K. H. Switak, respectively.

ANGOLAN PYTHON
(PYTHON ANCHIETAE)

A native of Angola and adjacent southwestern Africa, this serpent attains a length of only about 55 inches (about a foot in the newborns). They mate from October to February, and the female will lay a mere three to six eggs after about a 135-day gestation period. When breeding them in captivity, be sure to cool the males down to about 70°F before actual copulation and make sure the pair has plenty of privacy; this is an absolute must for this species.

The eggs should be incubated at about 85°F, with a humidity level of no less than 80%. The young should appear about 75 days later and can be sustained on a diet of pinkie mice.

One final note: The Anoglan Python is somewhat rare and hardly ever seen in captivity.

BOELEN'S PYTHON
(PYTHON BOELENI)

These are reasonably small for members of the python clan—the adults rarely reach over 10 feet. They are native to New Guinea and breed from December to March.

When mating them in captivity, be sure the males have a short "cooling" period at about 70°F, and then give the pair a moss substrate and a large water dish. After a gestation period of around 135 days, the females will lay about three to six large

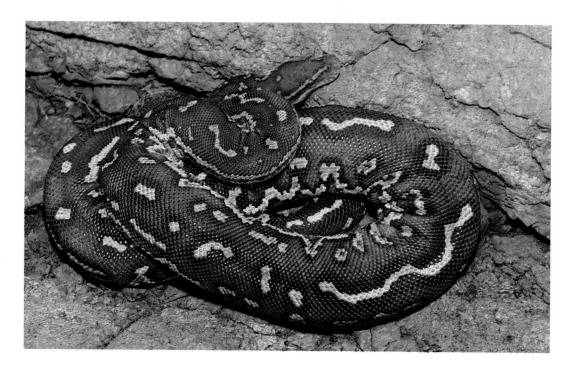

This beautiful animal is *Python curtus brongersmai*, a subspecies of the popular Blood Python . Blood Pythons are generally very short and powerfully built, and usually have a nasty temper. Photo by P. J. Stafford.

The Blood Python has been bred many times in captivity, the mother laying an egg clutch of about one dozen. Photo of *Python curtus breitensteini* by Jim Merli.

white eggs, which, if incubated properly (at 85°F and 80% humidity), should hatch in about 60 to 80 days.

The young, which will measure about 16 to 18 inches, should be given the same climatic conditions as the adults and sustained on a diet of pinkie mice or, less preferably, small birds.

BLOOD PYTHON
(PYTHON CURTUS)

Native to Malaya, Borneo, and Sumatra, this python breeds from December to March and attains a length of about 70 inches.

If you are breeding them in captivity, remember to cool the males down to about 70°F beforehand. The mother will have about 110 to 150 days of gestation before laying a clutch of anywhere from six to 15 eggs. These should be incubated at least 85°F and 80% humidity and will hatch about 75 days later.

The young will be about

one and a half feet in length and should be given ample quarters in which to hide. For their first meal, try feeding them pinkie mice and/or rats.

INDIAN PYTHON
(PYTHON MOLURUS MOLURUS)

The usual mating time for the Indian Python in its native India is from October to February. If you're planning on breeding them in captivity, be sure to cool the males down to at least 74°F beforehand. The females have a gestation period of 100 to 150 days, after which time a potentially large clutch of 12 to 60 eggs can be laid. Since the adults can attain a length of over 15 feet, they will need a large enclosure.

The eggs should be incubated at a temperature of no less than 85°F with a humidity level of at least 80%. Incubation lasts from 60 to 80 days, after which time the young, which should be about a foot long, will begin taking young mice and rats.

This snake is endangered.

BURMESE PYTHON
(PYTHON MOLURUS BIVITTATUS)

A popular pet species, the Burmese Python is an

The Burmese Python is undoubtedly one of the most popular of all the boids, and now an albino form has appeared. It commands a high price but is much in demand nevertheless. Photo by Jim Merli.

Many superb specimens of the Burmese Python, *Python molurus bivittatus*, like the one shown here, are now available in the herp hobby thanks to generations and generations of selective breeding. Photo by P. J. Stafford.

Some time in the past decade, a single albino Burmese Python, *Python molurus bivittatus*, entered the hobby, and now superb examples like this one are available, although not cheap. Photo by R. D. Bartlett.

enormous serpent—some can grow to well over 22 feet! Surprisingly enough though, this native of Burma, Malaysia, and Indonesia has very small young; they rarely measure over one and a half feet in length.

The Burmese Python mates from October to February and after a 110- to 150-day gestation period the females will lay a clutch of anywhere from one dozen to five dozen eggs. If you are going to try and breed a pair in captivity, the males should be cooled down to about 70°F before actual mating takes place.

Incubation of the eggs requires a temperature of at least 85°F, and a humidity level not less than 80%. This period will last about 60 to 80 days,

long as 10 feet. Their usual time of mating is from October to February. As usual, if they are to be bred in captivity, the males should be cooled down to at least 72°F before actual copulation takes place.

The time from mating to egg-laying lasts anywhere from 110 to 150 days, after which a clutch of seven to 15 will be laid. These should be incubated at about 85°F, with a humidity level of no less than 80%, for around 60 to 80 days. The young will be about 10 to 15 inches long and should be given ample hiding space (same as for the adults). Start them on a diet of pinkie mice as soon as possible.

OENPELLI PYTHON
(PYTHON OENPELLIENSIS)

A native of West Arnhem Land in Australia, the Oenpelli Python is extremely rare and highly

As time passes and more albino Burmese Pythons, *Python molurus bivittatus*, are bred, their prices will begin to go down and thus become more available to the average keeper. Photo by M. J. Cox.

and the young should be weaned on a diet of small mice and/or rats.

The Burmese Python is now becoming very popular in an albino form.

CEYLON (SRI LANKAN) PYTHON
(PYTHON MOLURUS PIMBURA)

Native exclusively to the small island of Sri Lanka, this animal can grow as

protected. The adults rarely attain a length greater than 12 feet and probably mate from December to March.

Not much else is known about this species's exact breeding habits, since it is almost never seen in captivity. However, it is safe to assume that the information relevant to other species occurring in the same climate, etc., can be relied upon with reasonable faith.

One thing known for sure is that their eggs have a reasonably short incubation period (sometimes as little as two weeks). The metabolism

rate in the adults is very high.

BALL PYTHON
(PYTHON REGIUS)

Another very popular pet species, the Ball Python can be expected to grow to only about 60 inches. It is native to Central Africa and mates from October to February.

The average gestation period is about 100 to 120 days, after which time one to eight eggs will be laid. To properly incubate these eggs, you should keep them at a temperature of at least 85°F, with a minimum 80% humidity. The young, which will

Notice the color variation between these two Ball Pythons, *Python regius*. Both photos by R. D. Bartlett.

The young of the Reticulated Python, *Python reticulatus*, are already 2 feet long at hatching. Photo by W. Wuster.

For the breeder, Reticulated Pythons, *Python reticulatus*, are among the easiest to propagate. They have a 135-day gestation period and clutches of eggs that number in the dozens. Photo by Roberta Kayne.

measure anywhere from 8 to 10 inches, should be provided with ample hiding places as they are very secretive. Feed them on a diet of small mice. A light color phase of the Ball Python now exists.

RETICULATED PYTHON
(PYTHON RETICULATUS)

A native of India, the Philippines, and Southeast Asia, the Reticulated Python long has been in contest with the Anaconda as to which one is the largest snake in the world. An adult Reticulated can grow as long as 35 feet, making it longer than the Green Anaconda (32 feet maximum), but the anaconda is a much heavier snake. Newborn Reticulates are already over 2 feet long when they emerge from the egg.

If you are attempting to keep one of these giants in captivity, be sure to give them proper-sized housing and frequent meals. Breeding males need to be cooled down to about 70°F before copulation. The females have a gestation period of about 135 days.

The eggs, of which there will be anywhere from 15 to 60, should be kept in a temperature of at least 85°F, with the humidity at about 80%. Incubation

lasts around 70 days. The neonates should be given small mice at frequent intervals.

As with the Ball Python, a light color phase of this species also exists.

AFRICAN ROCK PYTHON
(PYTHON SEBAE)

As one might have guessed, the African Rock

One of the complaints about Reticulated Pythons, *Python reticulatus*, is that they tend to be somewhat irascible. Photo by P. J. Stafford.

Python is native to Africa. It is a very large serpent, attaining a length of up to 20 feet. It mates from August to December in its native territory.

If you are going to try breeding the Rock Python in captivity, you should know that the males need to be cooled to about 70°F beforehand. A large enclosure is also required, as is a nice, secure hiding place.

After a 135-day gestation period, a clutch of anywhere from 15 to 60 eggs will be laid. These should be incubated at a temperature of not less than 85°F and a humidity level of about 90%. In 60 to 80 days they will hatch, producing a litter of 18- to 20-inch young. They should be given small mice and/or rats for their first meal.

TIMOR PYTHON
(PYTHON TIMORENSIS)

A native of the Timor and Flores Islands, this serpent is relatively small for a python: 60 to 81 inches. It breeds from August to December and has a gestation period of anywhere from 110 to 150 days.

When breeding them in captivity be sure to cool the males down to about 70°F before actual copulation. Then give them about 60% humidity and they will do the rest.

The eggs, which should number about six to 15, should be incubated in at least 80% humidity, with a temperature of no less than 85°F. After about 70 days, a litter of 12 to 16-inch young will appear. These should be sustained on a diet of pinkie mice.

Since the Reticulated Python, *Python reticulatus*, grows to such an enormous length, a keeper should consider space requirements before acquiring one. Photo by K. T. Nemuras.

Corallus caninus, Photo by A. van den Nieuwenhuizen.

Facing Page: Two color variations of the rare and beautiful Rock Python, *Python sebae*. Top photo by R. D. Bartlett, bottom by W. R. Branch.

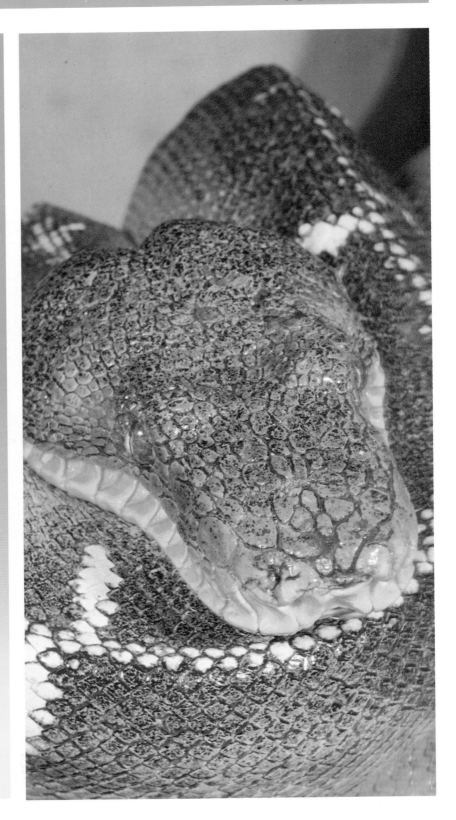

ENVIRONMENT CHART

Genus (Common Name)	Cage	Temp. (°F)	Humidity	Other
Acrantophis (Dumeril's Boa)	B & E	78-82	S & WB	H
Boa constrictor (Common Boa)	B & E	80-85	S & WB	H, T
Candoia (Pacific Boas)	B	80-85	S & WB	BW, T,H
Charina (Rubber Boa)	B & W	75-80	S & WB	BW, H
Corallus (Tree Boas)	E*	80-85	S & M, K	T, P, S
Epicrates (So. Am Boas) (Rainbow)	E (B)	78-85	S & WB	T, H
Eryx (Sand Boas)	D	85-90	WB	BW,H,O
Eunectes (Anacondas)	E*	80	S & WB+	P,T,O
Lichanura (Rosy Boa)	B	79-80	S & WB	H,BW
Sanzinia (Madagascan Tree Boa)	E*	80-85	S & M, K	T,P,H
Tropidophis (Dwarf Boas)	W & B	80-85	WB	BW,H
Ungaliophis (C. Am. Dwarf Boas)	W & B	80-85	WB	H,T
Aspidites (Black-headed Python)	B	80-85	WB,S	H,BW

Genus (Common Name)	Cage	Temp. (°F)	Humidity	Other
Bothrochilus [Liasis] (Ringed Python)	W	80	WB,S	H,P
Calabaria (Calabar Python)	W	75-85	WB,S	BW
Chondropython (Green Tree Python)	E*	80	S,M,K	T,P
Liasis (Australian Water Pythons)	E*	85	S,M,K WB+	P,H,)
Liasis (Children's and Pygmy Pythons)	W	85	WB,S	H
Liasis/Morelia (Australian Desert Pythons)	D	85-90	WB	BW,H
Morelia (Diamond Carpet Pythons)	W	85	WB,S	H,P
Python (Amethystine, Boelen's, Blood and Timor Pythons)	W	85	WB,S	H,P
Python (Indian and Reticulated Pythons)	E	80-85	WB+	H,P,O
Python (African Pythons)	B & W	80-85	WB,S	H

KEY:
B = BASIC
W = WOODLAND
E = EXTENDED
E* = LG. WOODLAND
D = DESERT

WB = WATER BOWL
S = SPRAYING
M = MISTING SYSTEM
K = HIGH HUMIDITY
WB+ = SWIMMING

BW = BURROWING
T = BRANCHES
H = HIDING
P = PLANTS
O = OPEN AREA

The Rainbow Boa, *Epicrates cenchria*, is one of the most terrestrial members of its genus and currently contains nine subspecies. Photo by B. Kahl.

Appendix

CHEMICALS AND MEDICATIONS

Oral Electrolyte Solution
Composition: Sodium chloride, sodium citrate, potassium citrate, calcium chloride, magnesium chloride, and sodium bicarbonate. Dextrose and vitamin C are added to some solutions.

Preparation: Keep refrigerated when not in use—warm to room temperature before using. Administered orally, although some preparations are sterile and can be given by injection (Lactated Ringers, U.S.P.).

Uses: Indicated for use in replacement of fluids and electrolytes for dehydration. Vitamins, minerals, and liquid meat and vegetable preparations can be added to these solutions to make nutritionally complete solutions for use in the feeding of young or unhealthy reptiles.

Diamond Python subspecies, *Morelia spilotes spilotes*. Photo by P. J. Stafford.

Diamond Python subspecies, *Morelia spilotes variegatus*. Photo by Roberta Kayne.

Cautions: Can cause fluid and electrolyte overload and gastric disturbances if administered too hot or cold, too rapidly, or in excessive amounts.

Multivitamin Supplements
Composition: Varying amounts of the essential vitamins, minerals, amino acids, and electrolytes. Most concentrated formulas contain all the vitamins, including vitamin D3, as well as balanced ratios of calcium and phosphorus if they are specifically made for reptiles. Regular vitamin supplements made for human consumption do not contain appropriate amounts of the vitamins and minerals that reptiles need, so they should not be used unless prescribed by a physician.

Uses: Indicated for use as a routine vitamin supplement as well as in malnutrition and dehydration.

Preparation: Powdered forms sprinkled on food items or added to nutritional and fluid preparations. Liquid forms are administered in the water and changed daily.

Cautions: The over-use of these preparations can cause vitamin and electrolyte imbalances, so only small amounts should be used, and they should not be given on a daily basis.

Povidone/Iodine
10-12% antiseptic solution
Composition: Active ingredient: 1% iodine; other ingredients: citric acid and glycerin.
Uses: Indicated for use in the cleaning of wounds and skin areas prior to antibiotic treatments and surgical incisions. Kills bacteria present on the skin.
Preparation: Dilute 5 cc (1 teaspoon) of povidone/ iodine solution with 20 cc (4 teaspoons) sterile water. If preferred, it can be diluted with only 15 cc of water for a more concentrated solution. Full strength povidone/iodine solution is used in surgical skin preparation. The solution is swabbed onto affected skin surfaces in small amounts. Also used on the mucus membranes of the mouth in very small amounts, but the solution is not to be swallowed, since toxicity can result.
Cautions: For wound care, this preparation should be diluted to lower the potential for iodine toxicity.

Neosporin Ointment
Composition:
Neomycin sulfate. There are several ointments that contain neomycin in different amounts along with other antibiotics such

as bacitracin zinc and polymyxin B sulfate within the ointment.

Uses: To promote healing and as a protective barrier for skin lesions and wounds. For topical application only. Thoroughly clean the affected area(s) first, then apply a small coating of this ointment to the wound one or two times daily.

Yellow Anaconda, *Eunectes notaeus*. Photo by B. Kahl.

Cautions: Use only a thin coating on the wound, and do not use internally.

Household Bleach

Composition: Hypochloric acid and water.

Uses: As a disinfectant for exhibit cages, incubators, water receptacles, and any other supplies used around reptiles.

Preparation: To make a dilute solution, mix one ounce (30 cc—6 teaspoons) of household bleach in 10 to 12 ounces of water. Clean all surfaces thoroughly with this solution, allow to dry for 30 minutes, then rinse at least three times, until no residue is present. If used on wood, rinse immediately so that the bleach solution does not soak into the wood.

Cautions: This solution must not be used directly on living tissues, since it is highly toxic. The available solutions must be diluted and rinsed completely from the surfaces of the supplies cleaned.

Sevin Garden Dust

Composition: Active Ingredient: Carbaryl insecticide (1-napthyl N-methylcarbamate 5%).

Uses: For elimination of mites and ticks.

Madagascan Tree Boa, *S. madagascariensis.* Photo by K. H. Switak.

Madagascan Boa, *Acrantophis madagascariensis.* Photo by Roberta Kayne.

Facing Page: Brown Sand Boa, *Eryx johnii.* Photo by B. Kahl.

Cautions: Should not be placed in or around water nor be ingested. Should not be used with neonates, juveniles, or small, delicate snakes.

Pest Strips/Fly Catchers
Composition: Rosin, rubber, and mineral oil on paper and/or tape. Some brands contain insecticides.
Uses: To catch flies, fleas, and other insects.
Preparation: Warm unopened tube in hands, then pull cord with a swirling motion, pulling strip out from casing. Hang in a brightly lit area, but not in direct sunlight

or excessive heat. Keep out of reach of children, and do not place where animals may come into contact with this item.
Cautions: Should never be used inside the vivarium or hung over the reptile's water source.

Sodium Sulfamethazine
Composition: Sodium sulfamethazine and water, 12.5% solution.
Uses: Antibacterial solution for the treatment of bacterial skin and mucus membrane wounds and lesions.
Preparation: Use full strength solution and apply with sterile cotton

swabs or gauze.

Cautions: Use only small amounts and for short durations (max. 14 days). Can be toxic, especially affecting the development of eggs. Use only on the skin, do not allow the reptile to ingest this product. If symptoms persist, consult a veterinarian.

Ampicillin

Uses: This is a broad-spectrum antibiotic for use in treatment of bacterial diseases caused by most gram-positive and gram-negative organisms. Can be used as a preventative treatment prior to surgery or other conditions that make the snake more susceptible to infection.

Preparation: May be given by injection, but can also be mixed with fluids and/or food and given by mouth. Ampicillin comes in powdered forms and must be diluted usually with 5 cc (1 teaspoon) of sterile water per 500 mg of ampicillin sodium.

Cautions: Must be diluted, the appropriate dosage calculated based on weight and general condition. A veterinarian should be consulted, since this medication has to be prescribed by a licensed practitioner. The over-use of antibiotics can cause secondary

Timor Python, *Python timorensis*. Photo by R. D. Bartlett.

Almost "patternless" Burmese Pythons, *Python molurus bivittatus*. Photo by W. P. Mara.

infections to develop due to the destruction of the normal bacterial colonies needed within the body, such as in the digestive tract.

Hydrogen Peroxide Solution
  Composition: Hydrogen peroxide (H_2O_2) 3% in water.
  Uses: For cleaning and disinfecting of skin and mucus membrane lesions and wounds.
  Preparation: Can be used full-strength or diluted with an equal amount of sterile water (1:1 solution). Apply to affected areas with sterile cotton swabs or gauze. Not to be taken internally. Application will result in effervescence (bubbling), but this effect is harmless.
  Cautions: As with all medications, this should only be used in small amounts, and only on an occasional basis.

Vitamin C, Ascorbic Acid
  Composition: Varying amounts of ascorbic acid (usually 50 to 1000 mg per tablet or per teaspoon of powder).
  Uses: Used in conjunction with antibiotics, electrolyte solutions, and fluids for replacement therapy for dehydration and malnutrition, as well as for supportive therapy for diseases and injuries that result in stress.

Green Tree Python, *Chondropython viridis,* "blue phase." Photo by K. H. Switak.

Facing Page: (top) Jamaican Boa, *Epicrates subflavus;* (bottom) *Candoia aspera.* Photos by R. D. Bartlett and K. H. Switak, respectively.

Preparation: Usually diluted in water or electrolyte solutions and administered orally. The powdered forms are preferred, but the tablets can be crushed to a fine powder as well.

Cautions: Protect from light and extreme cold.

Eucalyptus Oil
Uses: For the relief of respiratory distress due to the swelling and inflammation of the mucus membranes and tissues of the trachea and bronchi.

Preparation: Is a common ingredient in several types of topical ointments and aromatic rubs, it is used full-strength and applied in very small amounts to the areas just above the pits on the head of the snake.

Glossary of Terms

ARBOREAL: Tree-dwelling.

CAPSULE: A membrane enveloping another structure. Capsule of eye: the elastic or scale-like structure that protects the lens of the eye.

CLOACA: The passage and outer opening through which urine, feces, and reproductive fluids are discharged. Vent.

CLUSTER: Referring to eggs that adhere together during the incubation process.

COLD-BLOODED: Referring to an animal whose metabolism and body temperature are dependent on outside (environmental) heat sources.

CONTAGIOUS: Capable of being transmitted from one individual to another.

Blood Python, *Python curtus*. Photo by Roberta Kayne.

Rubber Boa, *Charina bottae*. Photo by R. D. Bartlett.

COMMUNAL: Referring to a community of several individuals.

COPULATE/COPULATION: To unite in sexual intercourse.

DEBILITATION: Loss of strength; weakness.

DEFECATION: The act of eliminating waste through the cloaca.

DEHYDRATION: The condition resulting from excessive loss of body water.

DISINFECT: To purify from organisms that cause infection; to clean thoroughly. A disinfectant is a chemical compound that cleans and purifies.

DIURNAL: Pertaining to the daytime; a diurnal reptile is most active and/or hunts for food during the day.

DOMINANT/DOMINANCE: To have a controlling influence.

DORSAL: Pertaining to the back portion; opposite of ventral.

ECDYSIS: Shedding or molting of the old skin after the new skin develops underneath. *Dysecdysis* refers to incomplete or improper shedding.

ECOSYSTEM: The complete system of living organisms and non-living elements that interact together in a specific area.

ELECTROLYTES: Substances found in the body that break down to form ions in solutions which are then capable of conducting electrical impulses—essential components of nerves and other cells.

EMACIATED: A condition in which the body is wasted or thin.

EMBRYO: The earliest stage of a developing fertilized egg that will eventually become the offspring. This term particularly describes the time of most rapid growth.

EMBRYONIC SAC: The membrane-like covering in which the embryo/fetus develops.

ENTRAILS: The internal organs.

FAST: To do without food.

FECES: Solid waste excreted from the bowel.

FERTILITY: Pertaining to the ability to conceive offspring.

FERTILIZATION: The union of the male and female reproductive cells, leading to the development of a new individual.

FETUS: The developing young in the later stages

of development up until the time of birth.

FLUORESCENT LIGHT: A tubular-shaped bulb containing a special chemical coating that produces light when an electrical current is applied.

FULL-SPECTRUM ULTRAVIOLET LIGHT: A specially designed fluorescent bulb that

emits all of the wavelengths of light necessary for the health of reptiles.

GENE: The chemical unit of heredity responsible for producing specific traits in the developing offspring.

GENETICS: The study of heredity.

GENUS: A group of related species; usually the first word in a scientific name.

GESTATION: The period of the development of young (pregnancy) and/or eggs inside the body.

GIRTH: The measurement around a cylindrical object; especially the measurement around the waist.

GRAVID: Pregnant or containing eggs.

Subadult Brown Sand Boa, *Eryx johnii*. Photo by Jeff Wines.

Vine Boa, *Epicrates gracilis*. Photo by R. D. Bartlett.

Facing Page: (top) Garden Tree Boa, *Corallus enydris*. (bottom) Rainbow Boa subspecies, *Epicrates cenchria alvarezi*. Photos by Michael Cardwell and R. D. Bartlett, respectively.

HEMIPENES: The organs of reproduction in male snakes.

HEREDITY: The genetic transmission of a particular trait from parent to offspring.

HERPETOLOGY: The study of reptiles and amphibians.

HIBERNATION: The dormant state of reduced metabolism which certain animals succumb to during the winter.

HUMIDITY: The amount of moisture in the environment.

HUSBANDRY: Management or care of living things.

HYDRATION: The absorption of water by the body.

IMPACTION: Being wedged in firmly; the overloading of an internal organ, such as the intestine; inability of the eggs to correctly move through the reproductive tract.

INCANDESCENT BULB: A bulb that emits light and heat derived from an electrical current and applied to a metal filament within the glass bulb.

INCUBATION: The process through which eggs are heated until the offspring hatch.

INFERTILITY: The inability to produce offspring.

INFERTILE EGGS: Eggs containing no developing offspring.

JUVENILE: A young animal; prior to becoming an adult.

LATERAL: Pertains to the sides.

LESION: An injury or breakage of the skin; includes blisters and abscesses, which are skin eruptions filled with fluids or pus.

LETHARGY/LETHARGIC: Drowsy, dull, lifeless, weak.

LUKEWARM WATER: Moderately warm to touch; approximately 70 to 80°F.

MALNUTRITION: The state in which an animal has received faulty or inadequate nutrition.

METABOLISM: The physical and chemical processes involved in the breakdown of food into energy, and the development of stores of chemicals within the body for use during growth and development of tissues.

METABOLIC RATE: The rate in which food ingested is broken down into energy for use by the body.

MISCARRIAGE: The loss of offspring from the body of the mother before they are able to survive independently.

MUCOUS MEMBRANE: The passages connecting to the outside openings in which the lining is

made up of cells that produce mucus; the oral cavity, the air passages, the upper digestive tract, the rectum, etc.

NECROSIS/NECROTIC: Death of individual or groups of cells, or of specific areas of tissue. Another term, "cheesy", is used to describe cell death in which the

Newborn Cook's Tree Boa, *Corallus enydris cooki*. Photo by P. J. Stafford.

tissues resemble cottage cheese.

NEONATE: Newborn.

NOCTURNAL: Pertaining to the night; a nocturnal animal is most active and/or hunts at night.

NODULE: A lesion that appears as a small lump or knot.

OOCYTE: An egg that has not yet reached full development.

OPAQUE/OPACITY: Having no luster; dull or cloudy.

OVULATION: The formation and release of the ovum (egg cell) prior to fertilization.

PARASITE: An organism that lives on or in another organism at whose expense it receives nourishment.

PHOTOPERIOD: The

amount of daylight hours versus the night hours the animal experiences.

PREY: Any animal that is caught by another for food.

PROBING: Technique in which sex is determined by measuring the internal sheath containing the reproductive organs with a metal or plastic rod.

PROPAGATION: Reproduction; to multiply by breeding.

REGURGITATE: To vomit partially digested stomach contents by way of the mouth.

REJUVENATE: To replenish or return to a normal state.

RODENTS: Mice, rats, squirrels, etc.; mammals with gnawing, ever-growing incisor teeth.

SANITIZE: To make clean and healthy by washing, scrubbing, disinfecting, or sterilizing.

SEXING: To determine the accurate sex of an individual.

SHEATH: A tubular envelope of tissue containing a body part or organ

SPERM: The male reproductive cells that fertilize an egg during breeding.

SPHAGNUM MOSS: Bog or peat moss. Useful for moisture retention.

STERILE: 1. Having no reproductive power; barren. 2. Free from microorganisms (bacteria/viruses).

STRESS: The biological changes that occur in the body as a result of adverse external influences, such as the need to defend against injury or damage.

SUBSTRATE: The bottom materials in a cage on which the animal rests; the "bedding."

TOPICAL: Pertaining to a particular area; a substance applied to a specific area of skin, which affects only the area it is applied to.

TRAUMA: A wound or injury.

VENTRAL: Pertaining to the abdominal or belly surface.

VERMICULITE: A substance derived from the heating of mica. Useful for moisture retention.

VESTIGIAL: Remnant of a structure that functioned in a previous stage of individual or species development.

VIVARIUM: A place where living specimens are maintained and raised; terrarium.

WARM-BLOODED: A body that can maintain a uniform temperature without depending on external heat sources.

Juvenile Rough-scaled Sand Boa, *Eryx conicus*. Photo by P. J. Stafford.

About the Authors

Erik D. Stoops of Scottsdale, Arizona, is an experienced specialist in the care of boas and pythons in captivity. He has taken his ten years of experience with collecting and maintaining reptiles and amphibians and developed an expertise in educating others new to the field of herpetology through lectures, video productions, and other presentations, based on his own experiences and knowledge. His personal goal is to continue to further his own education and experience in the field of herpetology by pursuing graduate degrees in biology and zoology, and to eventually become curator of a museum dedicated to the research and preservation of the reptiles and amphibians of the world.

Annette T. Wright of Phoenix, Arizona, is a registered nurse as well as an experienced specialist in the care of boas and pythons in captivity. She applies her nursing knowledge and skills toward the raising of neonates and the rehabilitation of reptiles with health problems. She shares her five years of experience with others who are new to the field of herpetology through participating in lecture and video presentations, as

well as discussion groups. She strives to promote understanding and compassion, as well as the sharing of knowledge and ideas, in the hope that more will be done to save the lives of the endangered species of all animals, particularly the reptiles and amphibians that are highly misunderstood.

Together, Erik and Annette work to educate the public—especially the children—about reptiles. Their personal approach and obvious respect toward the animals are the key to their success.

"Children will grow up believing what they are taught and what they see adults do, and we try to be role models for them so they can learn kindness

Boa Constrictor, *Boa constrictor constrictor.* Photo by P. J. Stafford.

Ball Python, *Python regius*. Artwork by E. H. Hart

and respect toward animals at an early age. We also try to give parents the true facts about reptiles, in order to decrease the general fear and hate that we so frequently see toward snakes in particular. Most of our future projects will be specifically targeted for children and young adults, since they are the ones who will be involved in the preservation and further study of reptiles in the future. Even now, children of all ages inspire both of us, since their curiosity and fascination are contagious and stimulate us to learn more ourselves.

"Understanding, caring, and hope are the philosophies that we incorporate into our lives, and what this book is all about."

Index

Page numbers in **boldface** refer to illustrations.